MW00411817

GREETINGS FROM ANGELUS

Poems by Gershom Scholem

Translated from the German
by Richard Sieburth

Introduced and annotated
by Steven M. Wasserstrom

archipelago books

These poems and Steven M. Wasserstrom's introduction
first appeared in Ibis Editions' *The Fullness of Time*, 2003.

Archipelago Books
232 3rd Street #A111
Brooklyn, NY 11215
www.archipelagobooks.org

Library of Congress Cataloging-in-Publication Data
Available Upon Request

Cover art: *Angelus Novus* by Paul Klee

Distributed by Penguin Random House
www.penguinrandomhouse.com

This book was made possible by the New York State Council on the Arts with the
support of Governor Andrew M. Cuomo and the New York State Legislature.
Archipelago Books also gratefully acknowledges the generous support of
the New York City Department of Cultural Affairs,
the National Endowment for the Arts, and Lannan Foundation.

PRINTED IN THE UNITED STATES OF AMERICA

GREETINGS FROM ANGELUS

Poems by Gershom Scholem

CONTENTS

THE FULLNESS OF TIME: SOME THOUGHTS ON THE POETRY OF GERSHOM SCHOLEM

Over your inconsistency, Lord,
Permit me that I brood:
You created the merriest poet of all—
And then you spoiled his mood.
Heinrich Heine

Gershom Scholem – philosopher, historian, unmatched philologist of Kabbalah, and one of the twentieth century's major scholars – wrote poems. His archives in Jerusalem contain some forty-five of these verses, in his own hand and in typescript. Scholem composed poetry sporadically throughout his life, from his early teens to his mid-seventies. Only two of the poems were published during his lifetime. This is, almost exclusively, private verse: intimate, oracular, reflective, light, melancholy.

The towering Jewish thinker early on exhibited a heroic determination to *become* Jewish. "Papa worked on Yom Kippur and didn't go to synagogue." With a sardonically Berliner edge, his father lit a cigar from the Sabbath candles with the blessing: "*borei pri tabacco*" ("Who creates the fruit of tobacco"). The sacrilege was not extraordinary, and not only in Berlin.

While the son seems to have understood his own character and destiny with almost freakish precision while barely into his teens, and though he wrote hundreds of pages from those days that survive, we still don't possess a rounded study of the life and works of the young scholar. Cynthia Ozick rightly "aches for a Thomas Mann to make a fat *Bildungsroman* of Scholem's early life...."

———

Patterns are traceable in the earliest records. Fortunately for the chronicler, Scholem sprang full-born, as it were, from the head of a Jewish Zeus. He was already rhyming "Golem" with "Scholem" (as Borges would do many years later) in verse recorded in his teenage journals. He transposed this megalomaniacal joke into various idioms, as when he told his mother he would attain the seventh level of heaven, or that he could perform alchemical feats of transformation, or that he would master Kabbalah, that most elusive and obscure of fields, which hitherto had been characterized by most liberal Jews as "degeneracy" and "impotent hallucination." It has only recently been discovered (since he left it out of all bibliographies of his work) that one of his first important scholarly publications was the 1928 "*Alchemie und Kabbalah*," in the occultist journal *Alchemistische Blätter*.

———

His first significant poem honored Theodor Herzl, to whom, in his volcanic early journals, Scholem compared himself in quasi-messianic terms. In one 1914 entry he invoked the figure of Moses as a model of devotion and leadership , then went on to quote Heine's lines about Yehuda Halevi: "Yes he will be a mighty poet...light and lamp to all his people, and a wonderful and mighty pillar of poetic fire." The figures of Herzl, Halevi, and the original poet-legislator – as Scholem refers to Moses in his notebooks – thus were all folded into the young Scholem's sense of his own vocation. As Moses redivivus, he reveals (concealed in his diary solitude) an ambition to storm the Kabbalistic heavens. To what extent this was to be allegory (the primary and predominantly rational figure of speech being studied by his friend Walter Benjamin), to what extent living, transcendent symbol (as he himself later concluded), he did not yet know. An oscillation between ascent and decent – "identification" and "distance" – set in between these poles.

The attraction of descent in particular was powerful. Jeremy Adler writes of Scholem's 1915 journal entry, on the Day of Atonement, where "he confesses that while he can fast, he cannot pray to God, but 'only seek Him.' He considers suicide, and 'breaks off relations with Heaven.' His problems with the Creator correspond to the discovery that he himself is not, after all, the Messiah. This entails an inward turn: 'the great event is silent, the eternal takes the path into the depths.'"

The weighty means for coming down to earth, for getting and staying grounded, turn out also to be strangely elevating. These means he called *philology*. As early as 1918, in a letter to his future wife Escha, he wrote that "philology is a veritable secret science."

—

The German milieu that elicited this esoteric conception of *Wissenschaft*, the philological science of Judaism, teemed with exaltations of *Dichtung*, poetry, and the argument can be made that Scholem's career as a master of German prose was in fact born in verse. For one, his epochal friendship with Walter Benjamin began with poetry, as the first writing Benjamin shared with Scholem was his essay "Two Poems by Friedrich Hölderlin" in 1915. Two years later, Benjamin praised Scholem's translation into German of the Song of Songs. And Scholem's first published scholarly article in his chosen field was "Lyric of the Kabbalah?" – which contains an excellent description of the mechanisms and effect of, for example, the mystical Hebrew "Poems of the Palaces," material that later found its way into his seminal *Major Trends in Jewish Mysticism*.

—

Private verse belonged to a venerable German tradition. In the last century, thinkers of the highest order (Jung, Benjamin,

Heidegger) continued to write poems that were not intended for publication, but were sometimes given as tokens of a certain kind of philosophical friendship.

———

His poems to Benjamin aside, perhaps Scholem's most revealing poetic work was written in the context of the intellectual circle known as PILEGESCH (Hebrew for "concubine"), an acronym formed from the first letters of the names of the six participants: Hans J. Polotsky, Hans Jonas (pronounced Yo-nas), Hans Lewy, George Lichtheim, Gerhard Scholem and Schmuel Sambursky. In the last months of his short life, the Berlin-born Jerusalem classicist Hans Lewy composed parodic verses in Latin for Scholem. Scholem then delivered the public eulogy for Lewy, in which he said that his late friend "possessed a poetic soul … and indeed the Muse's grace poured over him," then went on to talk of his friend's deep connection to poetry, and above al to the work of Stefan George. The physicist Schmuel Sambursky wrote several honorary poems to the Kabbalah scholar and to others in their circle, preserved in a rare volume titled *Nicht-imaginäre Portraits*. During this period, Scholem wrote affectionately satirical *Knittelverse* for his fellow Jerusalemite literati. Scholem's now-famous 1937 Hebrew letter to Salman Schocken, publisher of many of these learned friends, expressed Scholem's long-standing anxiety over the "professorial death" he had feared since his teenage years. He writes there of his "intuitive affirmation of those mystical theses that lie on the narrow boundary between religion and nihilism" and speaks of "the courage to risk the descent into the abyss that might one day swallow us up." Out of these intense relationships emerged what is perhaps Scholem's most important poem addressing his rather tortured vocation. "Vae Victus – Or Death in the Professoriate" was composed for Hans Jonas. "I have brought back the blurred face / Of the fullness of time. / I was ready to leap into the abyss, / But was I ready to make it mine?" However much Scholem by this point epitomized the magisterial philologist, his participation in a poetic community like PILEGESCH, scholarly as it was, hints at his having recognized the limitations of his science.

———

The poems are linked to specific events and ongoing conversations in Scholem's life, and they were almost always conceived as communications with friends. Yet – in a paradox that he no doubt appreciated – his deepest poems explicitly communicated a profound silence.

Silence is the eeriest *leitmotiv* of these poems. "He spoke for those ... devoured by silent grief" ("To Theodor Herzl); "Our words achieved only eloquence / As messengers of silence" ("The Ball"); "And the world is built / On your silence ... / I must carry what I feel within me in silence" ("W.B."); "Even silence is too hollow / Or too filled with righteous awe"

("For July 15"); Kafka's *deus absconditus*: "Should anyone dare inquire, / you would just stand mute" ("With a copy of Kafka's *Trial*"); "Ah, who could break this cursed silence, which carries him off, screaming in our ears" ("Bialik"); and the mysterious "But then all the silence / within the echo of these shrieks / erupts" ("Sirens").

What is this silence? It seems to be neither a failing of German nor an inadequacy of Hebrew, but rather a hole in the world. Scholem called it the *abyss*.

———

Nature makes no appearance in these poems. There is only history.

There is almost no Kabbalah, and certainly no "Judaism" in any conventional sense.

———

His favorite poets – tellingly, obdurately – remained German. We know this not only from his voluminous correspondence but from the meticulous catalogs he maintained for his beloved library. In 1923 he shipped 1,767 books with him on the boat to Palestine, including Rilke, Hölderlin, and the collected works of his favorite, Jean Paul. And he never broke this viscerally literary connection to the "Land of Poets and Philosophers" (*Dichter und Denker*). He cited Hölderlin and Goethe at climactic rhetorical moments of major public addresses. In his 1930 tribute to the preeminent Jewish theologian,

Franz Rosenzweig, he started and concluded with Hölderlin. He invoked Hölderlin again, on an equally instructive occasion – the 1961 completion of the Buber-Rosenzweig Bible translation.

———

While his masterpiece, *Sabbatai Sevi: The Mystical Messiah*, and numerous specialized works were composed in Hebrew, he wrote his memoirs, many of his major essays, and thousands of letters in German. So it should not surprise readers to discover that his chosen language of poetic expression was German.

———

Given his genius, the universal acclaim for his reach and achievement, it may seem petty to observe that this word-spanning man of letters was torn. Scholem's poems oscillate between the registers of *Trauer and Witz* – mourning and wit (or, as he put in a later speech, "the double impulse of severity and pleasure") – their polarity defining the ever-riven German Jew. Heine, Freud, and especially Karl Kraus, the edgy epigones of *jüdische Witz*, may be seen as his ironic precursors, even if he never explicitly acknowledged this debt.

———

As for *Trauer*, mourning, his preferred genre was the lament. In his teens he translated ancient and medieval Hebrew *kinot* (lamentations). His preoccupation with lamentations while Benjamin was writing his *Trauerspiel* (Mourning-Play) thesis set the darkening tone for their dialogue and inexorably evolved to engagement with Job and Kafka.

—

On the one hand, he said that Adorno "obviously lacked something Benjamin had – namely, a feeling for poetry." On the other hand – that of a dialectic or paradox – Scholem also insisted that a feeling for poetry as such was not enough for a scholarly conquistador (as Freud once referred to himself), and so his characterization of Buber's work as "poetry" was loaded, equivocal, unkind, but to the point. The real scholar cannot function as the poet does; the abiding significance of Kabbalah is revealed by means of philological rigor and unswerving rectitude.

—

Poetry nonetheless comprised one defining aspiration of many cultivated German Jews. George Moss, the historian of modern Germany, who knew whereof he spoke, once wrote an essay with the pregnant title, "Gershom Scholem as a German Jew." It is not difficult to discern in Scholem what Mosse identified as characteristic of the German Jew, that is, the prideful strains of *Bildung*. And one of the achievements of *Bildung* had to be poetry. This, despite the fact that, in his youth, he swelled with prophetic indignation against his German-Jewish peers: "Woe to the *Volk* that seeks rebirth through *Bildung*…. For this is your death-illness, you from the House of Israel, that you have too much *Bildung* and adopted too many of the evil ways of your lands."

———

Scholem received two major literary prizes. The bestowal upon him of the Bialik Prize in 1977 closed a circle in his life. Years before, in 1919, at the suggestion of Buber, he had published a German translation of Bialik's essay "*Halachah and Aggadah.*" On receiving the prize, he struck a note that resonated with this essay by the great Hebrew poet, elaborating the aesthetic richness of the Jewish mystical tradition: "The pictures, images, and symbols which grew upon this soil [i.e., Kabbalistic literature] or which fell upon these fields with abundance seemed to me to be filled with a poetic and lyrical significance, of equal worth to the theoretical meaning which I had set my mind to resolve." What he did not say on that occasion was that he once wrote a poem, in German, to Bialik, shortly after his death in 1934 (see page 81). A spare two quatrains, this lament drew its agonized theme of screaming silence from Bialik's other major essay, "Revealment and Concealment in Language," which contains the following lines: "For man shall not look on me and live,' says the void, and every speech, every pulsation of speech, partakes of the nature of a concealment of nothingness, a husk enclosing within itself a dark seed of the eternal enigma."

His reception of the literary prize from the Bavarian Academy of Fine Arts in 1974 occasioned several telling letters from his brother Reinhold. The two had long been out of touch, but in the early seventies they met up in Switzerland and their relationship resumed. Shortly thereafter Reinhold wrote to his now famous younger brother: "I don't know anything about your worldwide status in the scholarship of Kabbalah. Putting this aside, I see you, surprisingly, as a magnificent German writer." When word of the Bavarian Academy prize reached Reinhold two years later, he wrote his brother from Sydney, Australia, where he had been living since 1937: "[Y]our letter... arrived with the astonishing news about the literary prize from the Bavarian (!!!) Academy of Fine Arts. You'll perhaps recall what I wrote in the context of our discussion of Judaism: that, despite everything, you are a fine writer of German. I never expected that a German academy would confirm my opinion with a literary prize." Reinhold then noted the German epigraph to his brother's monumental *Sabbatai Sevi*, which states: "Paradox is a characteristic of truth. What *communis opinion* has of truth is surely no more than an elementary deposit of generalizing partial understanding, related to truth even as sulphurous fumes are to lightening." The author explained to his older brother that "the German quotation... (which you seem somewhat ambivalent about)... [is] in my humble opinion... an incomparable quotation, since it relates

to my own opinion on the nature of truth." Reinhold replies:
"The epigraph did not offend me; I simply saw it as confirma-
tion of how German your background is, when you, despite
all your Talmudic and Kabbalistic wisdom, used a German
citation on the 'partial understanding' of truth."

———

A link in the golden chain of poets from Heine to Nelly Sachs
and Celan. The place of Jewish poetry in German *Kultur*,
and the place of Jews in German poetry. It turns out that
Scholem was a German poet. Just as it has been said that
it was Jews who created the cult of Goethe, so it was these
at the ethnic periphery, Heine and Celan, who also belong
(somehow centrally) to that German canon. Scholem derided
the Jewish cult of *Deutschtum* (Germanness) and condemned
the bathetic delusion of a "German-Jewish symbiosis." Never-
theless – and in a sense that provocatively transcends all irony
– however lowly his position might be, this Israel too belongs
in the German pantheon.

———

There must not be any misunderstanding. Scholem vehe-
mently rejected as a dangerous delusion the wish-fulfillment
of *Bildung*. There was never, he insisted, any realistic possi-
bility that Germans would accept Jewish acculturation, no
matter how it was attained. The revelation of his German-
language poems does not belie his Zionism. "All in all," he

wrote in 1916, "I find myself in an advanced state of Zioniza-
tion, a Zionization of the innermost kind. I measure every-
thing by Zion.... The goal and meaning of life is called: Zion."

By 1921, however, already having adopted what Adler calls
"the enigmatic anarchism of his mature phase," he had sepa-
rated social and theological concerns. In a letter form Munich
written that year, Scholem identified "the fatal 'modern'
conflation of religious and political categories that desecrates
both, turning them into a game that someday is bound to
turn violent.... I... pledge my allegiance," he continues, "to an
utterly nonrevolutionary notion of Zionism – or one that can
be labeled revolutionary only with deep and nearly indecent
irony, since it refers to a stratum where there are no revolu-
tions. I do not think that the task of Zionism has any essential
relation to social problems.... I know only the deep continuity
of the Teaching [*Lehre*] – which has obviously faded from
Zion, though Zionists haven't noticed this." Adler notes that
Scholem's position hardened after he emigrated to Jerusalem
in 1923, and that "his disillusion led to despair."

In practice, Scholem's Zionism remained complex. He
consistently committed himself – in petitions, letters to
the editor, and other modes of persuasion – to reconcilia-
tion between Jews and Arabs. He belonged to the pre-State
group Brit-Shalom (The Covenant of Peace) and after the
Six-Day War felt that Israel's occupation of the West Bank
and Gaza was a grave mistake. He considered the settlers in

the territories yet another expression of Jews' "fatal attraction to messianism." On the other hand, he had long relinquished his idealistic dreams of the 1920s, as the disillusionment of these poems makes especially clear. His unshakeable vigilance regarding manifestations of anti-Semitism and the blandishments of assimilation – as in his almost hair-raising excoriation of *Portnoy's Complaint* – marked him as a stalwart Israeli patriot and cultural Zionist to the end. His identification of the absence of *ahavat yisrael* (love of the People of Israel) as the fundamental fault of Hannah Arendt's *Eichmann in Jerusalem* provided him with the *coup de grâce* administered in his assault on that book.

The poems' post-metaphysical resignation, then, does not refute Scholem's explicit theological proclamations elsewhere. "As I believe in God, I believe in the existence of absolute values....I don't understand atheists. I never did." That he maintained his attachment to secular German culture and remained both a believing Jew and a theological anarchist likewise does not rebut these putative confessions. Both sides, so to speak, express the truth. "Paradox is a characteristic of truth."

———

He was, as was differently said of his rejected father-figure Martin Buber, a bridge-builder. But he did not try and could not build bridges between German and Hebrew. He wrote poems in both languages, through the greater number (some ninety-five percent) and by far the best of them were in German; the disproportion between the work in each language is instructive for the historian. Like Buber, Scholem also translated from Biblical Hebrew into (pre-Nazi) German. In his *laudatio* to Buber in 1961 he acknowledged that "the German language...has profoundly changed in this generation." Their generation, which fled Germany, shared a nostalgia for the lost (pre-barbaric) German language of their youth.

———

His own poems are both stylistically and substantially old-fashioned. They are almost medieval, in the sense described by Curtius when he said that the medieval poet's mission was "to turn out compliments, epitaphs, petitions, dedications, and thus to gain favor with the powerful or correspond with equals." These verses are strictly purposive, crafted either to entertain or to teach; his Kafka poem was, as he described it to Benjamin, "a theological didactic poem...composed...for Kitty Marx's theological instruction." In 1968 he told George Lichteim that "herewith [in the poem about *The Trial*] my position in regard to blasphemy should be clearly expressed. Never and nowhere have I held a different position."

———

The Jerusalem philologist maintained contact with major writers throughout his life. The father of the modern Hebrew poet, Haim Nahman Bialik, strolled the streets of the new

Tel Aviv with the young scholar. In 1918 Scholem wrote an honorific sonnet ("Menashe Chayim") to his older friend, the novelist S.Y. Agnon, about one of the characters in an Agnon novel, and on the occasion of Agnon's seventieth birthday in 1958 he presented him with a hand-written copy. He delivered the eulogy for another poet-friend, "Lea Goldberg, Poet of Lonely Suffering." Even at the end of his life, he was demonstrating in detail to correspondents his intimate grasp not only of the poetry of a favorite of his youth, Rilke, but of the postwar Celan (whose career intertwined with that of Schoem in ways that remain to be elucidated). Late in life he told Irving Howe that he didn't have time to read "Israeli literature of the new generation," but, he said, "I highly appreciate Appelfeld....I think highly of Amichai and of Dalia Ravikovich in some ways. I appreciate less the others."

———

His pioneering investigations of Kabbalah would be unimaginable without the influence of radical thinking about language (*Sprachephilosophie*). Philosophers of language-Kraus, Rosenzweig, Benjamin – sharpened his focus and made it possible for Scholem to scrutinize the Zohar. Among the most self-reflexive and metaphysically obstreperous of texts, the Zohar presented Scholem with a language fit for a poet.

———

"What the value and worth of language will be – the language from which God will have withdrawn – is the question which must be posed by those who still believe that they can hear the echo of the vanished word of the creation in the of immanence of the world. This is a question to which, in our times, only the poets presumably have the answer." Scholem seems to suggest here that a philologist of Kabbalah would not have this answer.

———

George Steiner called him "the master of disenchantment." Scholem harbored no illusions, as a matter of principle and of pride. "The sheer illusion of the world / is now consummated to the full..../ no illusion here will hold" ("With a Copy of Kafka's *Trial*"). He could be scathing towards those who did cling to consoling fantasies – "Honor your illusions, / castles in the air!" ("To Mrs. Eva Ehrenberg"). For him, philology and the abyss were consolation enough, though they didn't provide all the answers.

———

There is no ecstasy here. He said of himself that he failed as a student of Kabbalistic poetics. In 1977, on accepting the Bialik Prize, the scholar reflected on his missed opportunities. He recalled his long-standing desire to unleash "the tremendous poetic potential" of the Kabbalah which he cherished as his "own secret longing."

———

A writer of poetry, if not, properly speaking, a poet, Scholem has exercised considerable influence on the world of poetry. It is hardly an exaggeration to say that nearly all modern Jewish poets interested even tangentially in Jewishness as such have read their Scholem – certainly Nelly Sachs, Paul Celan, Allen Ginsberg. The same may be said of literary critics, especially those of Jewish letters. Cynthia Ozick and Harold Bloom, Robert Alter and George Steiner, each in fundamental respects credits Scholem with their very sense of Jewish history. Even further afield, in music (John Zorn or new-wave klezmer) and the visual arts (Anselm Kiefer's series on the *Merkava* comes to mind), secularized "Judaic" high-culture of the twentieth century is for all intents and purposes Gershom Scholem.

———

The poems tell us that Zionism failed, that Scholem's own attempts at Kabbalistic "conquest" somehow failed, that the world is sliding away from itself into a darkening dissimilarity, leaving the seeming to cling to the vestige and then itself fall away. What Scholem in his later letters, interviews, and essays tells us is something very different. Though disillusioned with the redemptive potential of Zionism and Kabbalah, Scholem maintained a brave, confident, and wry demeanor when it came to facing the public. He took his responsibility – as prominent leader of Zionist culture, as pioneer scholar in Israel's leading university, as "Jewish thinker" – with the utmost gravity, if not with the ultimate sobriety once ascribed to Buber, i.e., messianic seriousness.

———

But Scholem did rededicate himself, with the rarest penetration, to difficult matters: to the cultural defense of his nation and his people, to maintaining the possibility of a living messianism, and not least, to the philology of Kabbalah. As philosopher he was both programmatically and fervently dialectical. His "dialectic" of Kabbalah and modernity was articulated in quintessential fashion in his Kafka poem. Kabbalah becomes non-Kabbalah. Loss, not untragically, becomes gain. What was central becomes marginal. What was once left out now occupies center stage.

———

There *is* ecstasy here. Extremes converge catalytically in this most unflinchingly honest of men, who – having endured suicides of intimate friends, the murder of a brother in a Nazi death camp, the ravaging of his Jewish homeland, the rapid decline of his Zion – knew the darkness of history. Tragedies in which meaning somehow transmuted itself, like loam, even as tiniest fertilizations of historical change. He believed in a "messianic" future, and he admitted in print, after a full half-century of intermittent disparagement, that the philosopher of Hope, his erstwhile friend, the nonagenarian Ernst Bloch, indeed was not wrong in affirming a secular, social messianism. Scholem kept looking ahead to a time when the order of things would be rectified. Pressed to clarify what a Kabbalah of this future might be, he noted that "what Kabbalists and other mystics revealed in their world" exists in the work of Walt Whitman. In other words, he claimed that poets in the secular realm might touch realities known to traditional Jewish mystics. Elsewhere he put it more emphatically: "William Blake can describe a world which resembles that of the Kabbalists."

———

If there is a historical discovery in these poems, it is twofold. First, that they express unequivocally Scholem's despair, at critical junctures, in the realization of Zionism – a notion that is fundamentally and even sensationally at odds with the image that the reading public has of him in this regard. Second, the poems shed light on a problem that has long preoccupied many a close reader of Scholem – that is, the relationship between the master's life and his work. For the poems, it would seem, show us that the professor was *not* a Kabbalist: a privately mystic Scholem is not recorded here. Of all his various genres – monographs, letters, lectures, essays, eulogies – the poems in fact might be the least mystical. His diaries are much more euphoric. If there is a consistent tone in the poetry it is neither that of esoteric secret-keeping nor of noetic *unio mystica*. The poems themselves are neither slyly reserved nor boldly synthesizing. Rather, they plunge us into the darker aspects of Scholem's vision – not into Kabbalistic practice so much as the starkness and often bleakness of the actual. Again and again the poems betray only estrangement, though Scholem notes that "In this estrangement we shall be free" ("Paraphrase, from the Prose of 'The Diary'"). Perhaps this isn't such a surprising finding after all for the man who announced that "where God once stood, Melancholy takes his place" ("With a Copy of... 'One Way Street'").

But there remains, at bottom, a shock in his choice of the language itself. Writing to Rosenzweig, Scholem expressed his sense that Hebrew should be reserved for "the revolution of a language," the "abysmal sublime." By comparison, his poetry in *German* is simply old-fashioned verse. Even when he invoked Hebrew as a foundation-shattering "volcano" (in the same 1926 letter to Rosenzweig), he did so in German. That so many of these most personal poems of young adulthood and middle age are written in the German of Scholem's youth and that they are preoccupied with disillusionment therefore may say the same thing: their very composition bespoke a failure of a sort. Moshe Idel has testified that Scholem was "in his own eyes, rather a failure, qua mystic." But the defeat and disappointment go deeper than that. His apocalyptic longing for the advent of a pure language was not answered in living Hebrew. Beyond estrangement from God and from Zion, he suffered estrangement from the Torah's language itself.

———

Born an old man, he had before he reached his twentieth year presciently and accurately grasped his life's program. He despised "the drug of self-delusion." In "Media in Vita," his mid-life confession, he states directly his sober creed: "I am uncannily attracted / by the darkness of this defeat; / since I no longer carry any banners, / I'm as honest a man you'll ever meet." The rejuvenations of clarity, the shock of dialectic, the German poet beyond Germany, the metaphysical Zionist disillusioned with political and actual Israel, the classical Hebraist discouraged by Hebrew realia, the Jew with his ancient eyes open and focused ahead, never forgetting the trajectory set in revelation, never neglecting the defeated, reviving the soul that confesses under the breath. Not, then, a "great poet," but one whose plainspoken dignity echoes profoundly through the verses finally printed here. In the fullness of time.

Steven M. Wasserstrom
Henderson, Nevada
June 2002

GREETINGS FROM ANGELUS

AN THEODOR HERZL!

Er war der erste, der die Worte sagte
Die uns erhoben zu den lichten Höhn,
Er war der erste, der das neue wagte,
Vor unseren Augen Niegeahntes ließ erstehn!

Er ging voran mit zukunftsfrohen Schritten
Und wies den Schwankenden die unbetretenen Bahnen!
Uns die wir bitter am Vergangnen litten,
Ließ er den neuen, bessern Frühling ahnen!

Er sprach für die die ihre Sehnsucht schweigen
An denen einsam frißt der stille Gram,
Sie alle hießen nun ihr Haupt sich beugen
Vor ihm, als zu den Hungrigen er kam.

Wir warden seiner nicht vergessen,
Der neu uns gab den bilderreichen Traum,
Der auferstehen ließ, was einstmals wir besessen,
War wir verloren—und wir fühlten's kaum!

Er schrie der Welt, die staunend sich erhoben,
Die Worte zu, die Worte unserer Not.
Er hielt uns hoch, unter der Feinde Toben,
Die Fahne, und die Fahne war blutrot!

Donnerstag, den 10.III.1915

TO THEODOR HERZL

He was the first to pronounce the words
That lifted us to the heights of light,
He was the first to dare a new world
That rose unsuspected before our eyes!

He preceded us with steps that gladly moved ahead
And showed untrodden paths to those in doubt!
To us who suffered from the past in dread
He pointed to a better springtime, a new way out!

He spoke for those who had repressed their longing
And for those devoured by silent grief,
And they all bowed their heads, now belonging
To him who had come to slake their disbelief.

We shall never forget what it was he meant,
Who gave us this dream so rich, so glowing,
And who restored what we had once possessed
And what we had lost—without our knowing!

He shouted of a world that rose, amazed
At his words, the words of our own distress.
He held the flag high as the enemy raged,
And the flag was bloody red.

Thursday, 10.III.1915

MENASCHEH CHAJIM

Du der das Leben sich vergessen macht
unsterblich ist es in dir auferstanden.
Da du in Not vergingst, in Schmach und Schanden,
bist du zur höchsten Ordnung aufgewacht.

Dein Dasein ward dem Schweigen dargebracht,
in das nur klagend unsre Worte fanden,
doch nicht wie unsere Klagen deine branden,
denn des Siloah Wasser fließen sacht.

Dein Leben steht im Licht der letzten Zeit,
aus deiner Stille Offenbarung spricht.
Unendlich groß erstrahlt in dir das Leid,
du aber bist das Medium das es bricht.
Und heißt solch Armut Leid und Irrsal nicht
Unschuld vor dem verborgenen Gericht?

MENASHE CHAYIM

You, who caused life itself to forget,
in you, immortal, life now resurrects.
Because you died in poverty and disgrace,
to the Highest Order you now awake.

Your existence was given to a silence
our words could enter only in lament,
but yours surged up unlike our sorrows,
sweeter than the waters at Shiloah.

Your life stands in the light of the Final Days,
out of your stillness Revelation has its say.
Grief shines forth from you, infinitely great,
yet you are the prism through which it breaks.
Come Judgment Day, will all this pain
and errancy bear Innocence as it name?

PARAPHRASE, AUS DER PROSA
DES "TAGEBUCHS"

von Walter Benjamin übertragen

Du wohnst allein in meinem Tagebuche
Und führst darin das unsterbliche Leben
Im Tode hat die Zeit dich mir gegeben
Daß ich in dir die Größe nicht versuche.

Die Landschaft wandelt sich zum Leichentuche.
Der Feind wird gegen mich sich steil erheben.
Und du, Geliebte, mußt dich ungern neben
Ihn stellen und verhindern, daß er fluche.

Jugend, du stirbst und bist doch die Historie
Aus deiner Liebe strahlt die Zeit als Glorie
Aus deinem Leben die Unsterblichkeit.

Die Zukunft war. Vergangenheit wird sein
Die Gegenwart wird uns vor Gott entzwein
In der Enfremdung werden wir befreit.

12 May 1918
Bern
nach der ersten Lektüre der
"Metaphysik der Jugend"

PARAPHRASE, FROM THE PROSE OF "THE DIARY"

after Walter Benjamin

You live alone in the diary of my life
Leading an immortal existence page by page
In death you have been given to me by Time
Lest I lose myself in you to things too great.

The landscape turns into a shroud.
The enemy will rise against me in a rage.
And you, Belovèd, alas must take your place
Beside him, lest he swear out loud.

Even as you die, Youth, you establish History,
From your love Time shoots forth it beams
And immortality blazes from your life.

The future was. The past shall be.
The present shall untwain us before God
In this estrangement we shall be free.

> *12 May 1918*
> *Bern*
> *upon first reading*
> *"The Metaphysics of Youth"*

ABSCHIED AN EIN JUNGES MÄDCHEN
An Greten

Unglück · Verschwiegen nur der Quell der Klage
In Deinem Leben ist es offenbart
Das Herz der Jugend ist in mir erstarrt
Die Lehre übergabst Du mir als Frage.

Dein abgewandtes Dasein hat die Tage
Die uns gefährden · Ruine · Mich bewahrt
Mein tiefstes Wissen strahlte Deine Art
In mich zurück daß ich es sehend trage.

Dein Wissen · Mädchen · ist das Unglück nur
Das niemand auf der Welt wie Du erfuhr.
Und Zion ist des Unglücks heilger Ort

Dorthin gehst einsam Du nun von mir fort.
Du Mitte mir · Wir müssen uns verlieren
Bis unsere Wege dort zusammenführen.

15.15.1918

FAREWELL TO A YOUNG GIRL
To Grete

Misfortune · The lament merely silenced at its source
In your life its well-spring is revealed
The heart of youth in me is now congealed
The Teaching you transmitted, a question I endorse.

Your face of Being, averted, contains the days
That place us at risk · Ruins · As my defense
The deep knowledge that should your presence
Dazzle me, I might stare straight into its rays.

Your misfortune · Girl · lies in knowing the truth
That no one on earth has so suffered as you.
And Zion is misfortune's most holy site

Toward which you now move, alone, leaving me behind.
You, my midmost self · We must lose ourselves before
Our paths lead that way, together once more.

15.15.1918

ZUM 15. JULI

Freund. Erwarte kein Symbol
das dir Größe künden soll.
Auch das Schweigen ist zu hohl
Und der rechten Ehrfurcht voll
Wäre Offenbarung nur
die mir niemals widerfuhr.

Deine Jahre sah ich nie
Ohne Staunen an, wie sie
Wuchsen in der Melodie
Einer reinen Phantasie
Die aus Gottes Mitte brach
Und die Lehre uns versprach.

Freund. Nimm dieses Zeugnis an
Das ich nicht zum Trug ersann
Tritt zu Dora hier heran
Aufgehoben sei der Bann
Der auf den Geschenken liegt
Sieh dich um und sei besiegt.

15.5.1918

FOR JULY 15

Friend. Expect no symbol
portending your greatness.
Even silence is too hollow
Or too filled with righteous awe
A revelation would be needed
at which I've never quite succeeded.

I have always gazed upon your years
Amazed how they appeared
To grow within the melody
Of a sheer fantasy
breaking out from the midst of God,
a promise of Teaching, and being taught.

Friend. Accept this as evidence
I had no deceit in mind
Take Dora by the hand
Let the ban on presents be deleted
Look around and understand
You've finally been defeated.

15.5.1918

DER BALL

Ich bin Jugend   du bist Freude
Aber Lüge sind wir beide
Wenn im Ball wir uns verlieren
Und uns selber pervertieren.

Wir verwerfen die Gemeinheit
Aber jene beßre Reinheit:
Freude in der Einsamkeit,
Von uns wiesen wir sie weit.

Jugend. Lachen ist nicht leicht
Wenn das Schweigen es uns reicht
Umkehr ist noch keine Flucht
Und gesegnet wer sie sucht.

Sprache die uns alles war
Bot sich nur im Schweigen dar
Freuden wir uns je zu zweit
Nahmen wir vorweg die Zeit.

Genius der Jugend, steige
Aus des Balles Wirrsal, schweige
Und dein Schweigen sei Gericht
Diese Jugend bin ich nicht.

15.5.1918

THE BALL

I am Youth   you are Joy
Yet both of us are lies
Too enthralled by the ball
To be ourselves at all.

We reject what is common
Yet have now forgotten
That finer, purer home:
The joy of being alone.

Youth. Laughter is hard
When all silence is barred
Yet turning back is no escape
Blessèd those who seek change.

Our words only took on sense
As messengers of silence
We only took joy in rhyme
Having forestalled time.

Genius of Youth, climb free
Of the giddy ball, cease to speak
And let your silence bear proof
I am not this Youth.

15.5.1918

W. B.

Trauernder, nah mir und doch stets verborgen
Nur die Berufung dich am Leben hält
Doch schweigst du. Auf dein Schweigen ist die Welt
gebaut. Die Trauer ist der ewige Morgen

In dem du stehst. Daß du noch nicht gestorben
das ist das Wunder das mich überfällt.
Du bist. Aus deiner tiefen Stille quellt
die Frage die dich mir, mich dir geworben.

Du warst bei mir in all den schweren Tagen
und bist doch fern bei dem der dich besaß
Was mich bewegt muß stumm ich in mir tragen.
Denn was an dir geschieht, hat solches Maß
der Größe daß die Worte die ich finde
nicht rein genug sind. Drum ist Sprechen Sünde

15 Juli 1918

W. B.

Mournful one, near to me yet ever remote
Only your calling holds you close to life
But you do not speak. And the world is built
on your silence. Mourning is the eternal dawn

You greet. And that you have not yet died
is a miracle that lies beyond my reach.
You simply are. And from your deep quiet
arises the question that binds us, each to each.

You who stood by me during my difficult days
are far from me who took you as his estate.
I must carry what I feel within me in silence.
For what you are going through is so great
that any words I might find to cast it in
would prove impure. Speech is thus a sin.

15 July 1918

GRUSS VOM ANGELUS
(Paul Klee "Angelus Novus")

W. B. zum 15. Juli 1921

Ich hänge edel an der Wand
und schaue keinen an
ich bin vom Himmel her gesandt
ich bin ein Engelsmann.

Der Mensch in meinem Raum ist gut
und interessiert mich nicht
ich stehe in des Höchsten Hut
und brauche kein Gesicht.

Der ich entstamme, jene Welt
Ist maßvoll, tief und klar
was mich im Grund zusammenhält
erscheint hier wunderbar.

In meinem Herzen steht die Stadt
in die mich Gott geschickt.
Der Engel der dies Sigel hat
wird nicht von ihr berückt.

Mein Flügel ist zum Schwung bereit
ich kehrte zurück

GREETINGS FROM ANGELUS
(Paul Klee "Angelus Novus")

To W. B., on July 15, 1921

I hang nobly on the wall
and look no one in the eye
I have been sent from heaven
an angelman am I.

Man is well within my realm
I take little interest in his case
I am protected by the Almighty
and have no need of face.

The world from which I come
is measured, deep and clear
what keeps me of a piece
is a wonder, as it here appears.

In my heart stands the town
where God sent me to dwell.
The angel who bears this sign
falls not beneath its spell.

My wing is poised to beat
but I would gladly turn home

39

denn blieb ich auch lebendige Zeit
ich hätte wenig Glück.

Mein Auge ist ganz Schwarz und voll
mein Blick wird niemals leer
ich weiß was ich verkünden soll
und weiß noch vieles mehr.

Ich bin ein unsymbolisch Ding
bedeute was ich bin
du drehst umsonst den Zauberring
ich habe keinen Sinn.

were I to stay to the end of days
I would still be this forlorn.

My gaze is never vacant
my eye pitchdark and full
I know what I must announce
and many other things as well.

I am an unsymbolic thing
I mean what I mean
you turn the magic ring in vain
there is no sense to me.

TRAURIGE ERLÖSUNG

Der Glanz aus Zion scheint vergangen
das Wirkliche hat sich gewehrt.
Wird nun sin Strahl, noch unversehrt
ins Innere der Welt gelangen?

Zu lange waren wir befangen
in dem was unser Herz begehrt
und der Vernichtung zugekehrt,
hassen wir nun, die uns verlangen.

Seele, du glaubst, du bist allein,
verfallen dem göttlichen Gericht
ob ungeglückter Tat. Du irrst.

Nie konnte Gott dir näher sein,
als wo Verzweiflung auch zerbirst:
in Zions selbstversunkenem Licht.

1926

MOURNFUL REDEMPTION

The light of Zion seems no more,
the real has now won the day.
Will its untarnished ray
attain the world's inmost core?

We have been mired far too long
in what makes our heart most race
and, staring annihilation in the face,
we hate those who seek our love.

Soul, you believe you are alone
and stand condemned in God's sight
for some failure on your part.

Wrong! God never comes more close
than when despair bursts into shards:
in Zion's self-engulfing light.

1926

AMTLICHES LEHRGEDICHT
der
Philosophischen Fakultät
der
Haupt- und Staats-Universität Muri

Von
GERHARD SCHOLEM
Pedell des religionphilosophischen
Seminars

Seiner
Magnifizenz
WALTER BENJAMIN
Rektor der Universität Muri
damals wie heute gewidmet
zum 5. Dezember 1927
vom Verfasser

THE OFFICIAL ABECEDARIUM
of
The Faculty of Philosophy
of
The State University of Muri

compiled by
GERHARD SCHOLEM
Beadle of the Seminar
on the Philosophy of Religion

To
His Magnificence
WALTER BENJAMIN
Rector of the University of Muri
as before so today this is dedicated
on December 5, 1927
by its author

A

Anfangs war zwar das Apriori
Aber selbst Alphons von Liguori
Argumentiert mit Hilfe des
Ältesten Aristoteles

B

Franz Baader pries uns Böhmes Licht
Brentano schätzte beide nicht
Unkontrollierbar schien ihm Tiefe:
Er liebte bündige Begriffe.

C

Wo Cohen redete in Zungen
Da ist Cassirer ihm entsprungen
Creiert aus dem Continuum
Von Cantor bis Cartesium.

D

Die Durée Bergsons trifft heut schon
Auf völlige Desillusion.
Nur Diltheys Name rettet D
Er ist dessen Deo-Dizee.

A

In the beginning was the a priori
But even Saint Alphonsus of Liguori
Made his casuistry equiprobable
With the help of old Aristotle.

B

Franz Baader praised Bohme's light
Brentano thought neither was right.
He always recoiled from the abyss:
He liked his concepts clean and crisp.

C

Where Cohen spoke in tongues
Cassirer was newly spun
Created from the continuum
Linking Cantor to Cartesium.

D

Nowadays Bergson's Durée
Elicits nary a hooray.
Only Dilthey's name, amen,
Justifies the ways of D to men.

E
Daß Eucken die Philosphie
Erneuert hätte, glaube nie.
Ob Euler starker Esser war
Die Frage scheint mir unfruchtbar.

F
Für Freud und Fichte fechten heute
Nur allzuviele faule Leute.
Man weiß von mancher falschen Fee
Mehr als von Michael Faraday.

G
Gabirol war ein großer Mann
Selbst Gobineau erkennt das an.
Wer Gundolf auf den Goethe kriecht
Bekommt die Georgianer-Gicht.

H
Wer heilig ist und hochmodern
Zugleich, halt es mit Husserl gern.
Doch hört man ein Gerücht im Land.
Daß Heidegger ihn nicht verstand.

E

Whether Eucken in fact renewed
Philosophy cannot be proved.
Whether Euler had a larger appetite
Is a question that does not sit quite right.

F

Too many lazy minds fight
For Freud and Fichte in our times.
We would sooner rhyme a virelay
Than observe the laws of Faraday.

G

Ibn Gabirol was a hero to his age
Even Gobineau agrees he was a credit to his race.
Whoever follows Gundolf on his Goethe route
Is sure to be afflicted with George's gout.

H

Whoever is ultramodern and ascetic
Will find Husserl most sympathetic.
Though there is a rumor going through the land
He was someone Heidegger could never understand.

J

Jamblichus war ein Obskurant
Von James ist solches nicht bekannt.
Doch macht auch Jaspers mit viel Kunst
Um ernste Dinge blauen Dunst.

K

Was nicht Begriff ist, ist konkret.
Endlich ein Satz, den man versteht.
Wo Kayserling im Klaren fischt
Wird Kant sehr leicht mit Kaut vermischt.

L

Von Leibniz spricht die Logik viel.
Lotze schreibt allzuleichten Stil.
Lichtenberg ist ein großes Licht.
Lambert und Liebert liest man nicht.

M

Mose ben Maimon schrieb den "Moreh".
Die Marburger machten Furore.
Metaphysik und Mengenlehr'
Für Mach sind Monstra nur, nicht mehr.

J

Jamblichus was utterly enigmatic
But James proves perfectly pragmatic.
Yet even Jaspers, in many artful ways,
Jams his ideas into the bluest of haze.

K

What is not a koncept is koncrete:
At last a sentence that's easy to read.
When Kayserling goes fishing for klarity
Kant and Kaut achieve a kind of parity.

L

Logic's debt to Leibniz is apparent.
Lotze's style is most transparent.
Lichtenberg's light goes to one's head.
Lambert and Liebert lie unread.

M

Moses ben Maimon meditated the "Moreh."
The Marburg School caused a great furore.
Metaphysics and number theory
Made Ernst Mach extremely leery.

N

Das Nichts, das ist der wahre Nus
Lehrte schon Nikolaus von Cues.
Von Nichteuklidik jeder spricht
Ob er es nun versteht, ob nicht.

O

Die Offenbarung Ostwalds trog
Okkam jedoch ist sehr en vogue.
Denn vielen gilt als dernier cri
Wieder einmal Ontologie.

P

Von Plato man schon früh erfährt.
Die Psychologen sind gelehrt.
Die Phänomenologen sind
Dafür beim Heil'gen Geist lieb' Kind.

Q

Die Qualitäten quellen wie
Uns lehrt die Quantentheorie
Aus Quatsch. Drum auch dies Alphabet.
So ungewöhnlich gut gerät.

N

All is nothing, all is naught
So Nicholas of Cusa taught.
Everyone talks of non-Euclidean space
Where whatever is is not the case.

O

Ostwald's latest opus is a hoax
Yet Occam is very much in vogue
For many consider it the dernier cri
To revert back to Ontology.

P

One learns of Plato early in life.
Psychologists are all learned types.
Phenomenologists are therefore those
Born full-blown from the Holy Ghost.

Q

Qualities, so quantum theory claims,
Can either be particles or waves.
This uncertainty just might be
The principle behind this ABC.

R

Der Raum ragt in die Welt hinein,
Riehl richtet reichlich sich drin ein.
Am Reinen, jenem Grundbeg-Riff
Scheiterte Avenarius' Schiff.

S

Aus Simmels Sitz sauste im Zug
Verzweifelt Sokrates. Er trug
Sehnsucht nach dem System. Die Bahn
Hält schon in Marburg an der Lahn.

SCH

Die Schlegel schrieben scharf und bloß
Mit Schiller wäre nicht viel los.
Lies scheint dir Schelling noch zu bunt
Dein kleinen Schwegler, nur nicht Wundt.

ST

Stifter kam Studien-halber in
Den Himmel. Stirner war schon drin.
Drob staunte er, zumal auch Sterne
Sich scheinbar gut stand mit dem HErrn.

R

The world projects itself as space,
And here Riehl takes pride of place.
This radical reality proving sound,
The ship of Avenarius runs aground.

S

Simmel's sociology is so complex
It leaves Socrates quite perplexed
If to systems you are drawn,
Next stop: Marburg an der Lahn.

SCH

The Schlegels, who rarely pulled a punch,
Said Schiller was surely out to lunch.
Should Schelling strike you as too blunt,
Read Schwegler, but never Wundt.

ST

Stifter went to heaven with no degree.
Stirner preceded him as all can see.
To his astonishment, even Sterne
Got in without waiting his turn.

T

Terror treibt manche Theorie
Durch feierliche Termini.
Jedes Problem: den Tod, die Zahl
Behandelt man transzendental.

U

Unsinn ist manchmal mathematisch.
Auch Ular ist uns unsympathisch.
Er urteilt ab in einem Satz
Die schwierigsten Upanischads.

V

Auch Vaihinger gehört zum Gros
Der Schwätzer, Volkelt ebenso.
Valete! Man vergißt euch bald!
Da hat doch Vischer festern Halt.

W

"Prinzipen der Wälzer" plant
Ein Wissender am Seinestrand.
Kommt dieses witz'ge Werk zustand
Klebt Wilhelm Wundt wohl an der Wand.

T

Terror drives much theorization
Into a tumult of totalization.
Whatever the problem, Death or Passion,
One solves it in transcendental fashion.

U

Unreason can be mathematically described.
Yet Ular is not sympathetic to our eyes.
All his logic-chopping never adds
One whit to the mysterious Upanishads.

V

Vaihinger has vaulted into the pantheon
As has Volket, who natters on and on.
Valete! You two will soon be obsolete!
I vote for Vischer, with my feet.

W

"All the Wisdom of the World" is planned
By a savant with much time on his hands.
When this witty work becomes available to all
Wilhelm Wundt will be nailed to the wall.

X

Ich glaube, daß Xenophanes
Den Xantner Ritualprozeß
Nicht mehr erlebt hat. Xenophon
Wär' jetzt Historiker in Bonn.

Y

Wer liest den armen Yorick nicht.
Young reizt schon eher zum Verzicht.
Der Yoga-Lehren wahren Fond
Erforscht Sir Arthur Avalon.

Z

Als Ruhe liebenden Zeloten
Zeichnen den Zeno Zellers Noten.
Ein großer Zaddik scheinet uns
Der vielzerzauste Lippmann Zunz.

X

Xenophanes was less than ecstatic
To be categorized as an Eleatic.
Yet Xenophon would glady be a don
In the History Department of Bonn.

Y

Alas, poor Yorick, we have read thee well.
Young's laws of optics can go to hell.
We would rather seek true oblivion
In the Yoga-lore of Sir Arthur Avalon.

Z

Zeller's essays show Zeno to be
A zealot who wished to live in peace.
No less zany, and certainly no dunce
Is the Jewish historian Lippmann Zunz.

BEGEGNUNG MIT ZION UND DER WELT
(Der Untergang)

Damals sind wir weggegangen
denn das alte Haus was so leer.
Wir hatten nur rein Verlangen
und nahmen den Weg nicht so schwer.

Und doch: vor jedem Hause
ein neuer Scheideweg.
Und wo wir immer standen
führte ein neuer Weg hinweg.

Wir aber waren fröhlich
wir hatten einen Plan.
Eine verborgene Hoffnung
hatt' es uns angetan.

Denn an den langen Wegen
schien Gott zu stehn.
Wir dachten: hier ruht Segen,
wir dürfen zu uns gehen.

Uns hat der Tag geschändet,
was wächst, braucht Nacht.

ENCOUNTER WITH ZION AND THE WORLD
(The Decline)

We left the place long ago
for the ancient house was bare.
We had but one thing in mind
and saw no problem getting there.

And yet: at every house
a new fork in the road.
Wherever we found ourselves,
another path to undergo.

But we were full of joy,
we had a plan in mind.
A most secret hope
made us so inclined.

For it seemed God stood
along this endless path.
We thought: blessèd is this way,
to ourselves it leadeth back.

We were harmed by light of day,
what grows has need of night.

Wir sind an Gewalten verpfändet,
An die wir nie gedacht.

Im Brennpunkt der Historie
sind wir verbrannt:
zerstört die geheime Glorie,
die zu sichtbar zu Markte stand.

Das war die trübste Stunde:
Erwachen aus dem Traum.
Und doch: die die Todeswunde
empfingen, merkten es kaum.

Was innen war, ist nach Außen
verwandelt, der Traum in Gewalt,
und wieder sind wir draußen
und Zion hat keine Gestalt.

23. Juni 1930

We stand in debt to powers
we never thought to invite.

History has focused its fire
on us and we go up in smoke;
gone is that secret splendor
in whose commerce we went broke.

This was the darkest hour:
waking from the dream.
And though the wounds were mortal,
they were never what they seemed.

What was within is now without,
the dream twists into violence,
and once again we stand outside
and Zion is without form or sense.

23 June 1930

AN MICH ODER SIE?

Betrögest du dich nur ums Licht
das aus dir selber scheint—
es wäre so vernichtend nicht,
wärst du dein eigener Feind.
Hier stünde ja, auf tieferem Grund,
dir noch ein Sieg bevor,
du schlössest mit dir selbst den Bund
verschlössest selbst dein Tor.
Wo Licht und Nacht in eins verlischt
im unentschiedenen Schein,
mit allem Lebenden vermischt
sammelst du selbst dich ein.
Gewähre, was du nie begehrt
verleugne was du bist
noch immer trätst du unversehrt
aus wesentlichem Zwist.
So vielfach könnte nie die Zeit
zerspalten sein, daß nicht
in höherer Besonnenheit
ihr Strahl sich an dir bricht.
Nur wo du dich behaupten willst
in sichtbarlicher Tat
nur wo du dein Verlangen stillst
begehst du den Verrat.

TO ME OR HER?

To cheat yourself of the light
that shines forth from you
would hardly reduce you to ruins,
were you your own enemy in the fight.
Indeed, it might even provide
a deeper ground for victory,
should you enter into a league
with yourself and bolt your gates.
Where Night and Light meld
into indeterminate seeming,
you blend with all living things
and gather yourself into your being.
Although you might give in
to what you've never desired
or disavow what you've always been,
you would still escape
this earthshaking conflict,
undamaged and undimmed.
Time could never be split
into so many bits that its light
refused to filter through to you
in a higher presence of mind.
But to choose to affirm yourself
in more visible forms of action

Denn dunkler war noch keine Nacht
als Zions Wirklichkeit:
das Sichtbare hat keine Macht
in innerlicher Zeit
denn sein geheimster Grund besteht
im Zwielicht der Magie
die Lüge der Identität
wer sonst vollbrachte die?

Frühjar 1931

or to silence your deepest demands,
would be a form of treason.
For no night was ever darker
than the reality of Zion:
the visible loses its power
when times turn more inward
for its most secret ground lies
in the twilight of magic—
how else could the lie of identity
ever have been achieved?

Spring 1931

MEDIA IN VITA

Ich habe den Glauben verloren
der mich hierher gebracht.
Doch seit ich abgeschworen,
Ist es um mich Nacht.

Das Dunkel der Niederlage
zieht mich unheimlich an;
seit ich keine Fahne mehr trage,
bin ich ein ehrlicher Mann.

Ich kämpfe für keine "Sache",
ich kämpfe nur noch um mich,
ich beziehe die einsamster Wache,
auf die noch ein Mutiger schlich:

Ich weiß nicht, ob ich sie bestehe,
Die Wache am Rand des Nichts
in der unendlich beklemmenden Nähe
des großen versunkenen Lichts.

Ich weiß nur: keine Entscheidung
ist mir mehr frei gestellt.
Ich möchte vielleicht die Verkleidung,
alles andre entscheidet die Welt.

MEDIA IN VITA

I have lost the faith
that brought me to this place.
And in the wake of this forsaking,
night is my surrounding space.

I am uncannily attracted
by the darkness of this defeat;
since I no longer carry any banners,
I'm as honest a man you'll ever meet.

I'm not fighting for any "cause,"
all I'm fighting for now is me,
I stand the loneliest of guards,
It takes courage to see what I see:

I don't know how long I'll hold my own
keeping watch on the edge of the abyss
in the stifling prospect of light
sunk into such an enormous pit.

All I know is that I am not free
to decide things for myself.
I could perhaps put on a disguise,
but the world decides everything else.

69

Die Welt? Oder nicht eher der Abgrund des Nichts,
in dem die Welt erscheint—
die Spiegelung des zweiten Geischts,
das mich unerbittlich verneint.

1930/33

The world? Or rather that abyss
of nothingness in which the world appears—
the reflection of that second face
ever eager to negate me here.

1930/33

MIT EINEM EXEMPLAR VON
WALTER BENJAMINS "EINBAHNSTRASSE"
(Kitty zur Hochzeit, 1933)

Ob dies das Landschaftsbild der Einbahnstraße ist,
die Ihr durchlaufen wollt?
Ich muß es fast bezweifeln. Aber wißt,
wohin Ihr sollt.
So viele Straßen haben Rückfahrtswege,
die man nicht sieht,
und kommt man mit der Richtung ins Gehege:
Es ist nicht wahr, daß einem nichts geschieht.
Bei Kollisionen wird hier nicht verhandelt.
Der Blitz schlägt ein.
Und findest du dich plötzlich ganz verwandelt—
es ist kein Schein.
In alten Zeiten führten alle Bahnen
zu Gott und seinem Namen irgendwie.
Wir sind nicht fromm. Wir bleiben im Profanen,
Und wo einst "Gott" stand, steht Melancholie.

WITH A COPY OF WALTER BENJAMIN'S "ONE-WAY STREET"

(to Kitty on her wedding day, 1933)

Is this the landscape painting of the One-Way Street
through which you'd like to stroll?
I almost doubt it. But know
where it is you ought to go.
So many streets have opposite lanes
one never sees,
and when you meddle with the way to take,
things are apt to eventuate.
You can't talk your way out of collisions.
Lightning strikes.
And should you find yourself suddenly quite transformed—
there is more than meets the eye.
In days of old all roads somehow led
to God and his name.
We are not devout. Our domain is the profane
and where "God" once stood, Melancholy takes his place.

MIT EINEM EXEMPLAR KAFKAS "PROZESS"

Sind wir ganz von dir geschieden?
Ist uns, Gott, in solcher Nacht
nicht ein Hauch von deinem Frieden,
deiner Botschaft zugedacht?

Kann dein Wort denn so verklungen
in der Leere Zions sein—
oder gar nicht eingedrungen
in dies Zauberreich aus Schein?

Schier vollendet bis zum Dache
ist der große Weltbetrug.
Gib denn, Gott, daß der erwache,
Den dein Nichts durchschlug.

So allein strahlt Offenbarung
in die Zeit, die dich verwarf.
Nur dein Nichts ist die Erfahrung,
die sie von dir haben darf.

So allein tritt ins Gedächtnis
Lehre, die den Schein durchbricht:
das gewisseste Vermächtnis
vom verborgenen Gericht.

WITH A COPY OF KAFKA'S TRIAL

Are we utterly estranged from you?
Lord, is no breath of your peace
or hint of your promised light
meant for us in this dark night?

Can your word have become so faint
among Zion's empty wastes—
or has it yet to permeate
this spellbound realm of of semblance?

The sheer illusion of the world
is now consummated to the full.
Lord, grant that he may awake
whom your absence has erased.

This is the sole ray of revelation
in an age that disavowed you,
entitled only to experience you
in the shape of your negation.

Memory can now only draw
on the Teaching that breaks semblance
apart: the expected settlement
from the remote court of law.

Haargenau auf Hiobs Waage
ward gemessen unser Stand,
trostlos wir am jüngsten Tage
sind wir durch und durch erkannt.

In unendlichen Instanzen
reflektiert sich, was wir sind.
Niemand kennt den Weg im ganzen,
jedes Stück schon macht uns blind.

Keinem kann Erlösung frommen,
dieser Stern steht viel zu hoch,
wärst du auch dort angekommen,
stündst du selbst im Weg dir noch.

Preisgegeben an Gewalten,
die Beschwörung nicht mehr zwingt,
kann kein Leben sich entfalten,
das nicht in sich selbst versinkt.

Aus dem Zentrum der Vernichtung
bricht zu Zeiten wohl ein Strahl,
aber keiner weist die Richtung,
die uns das Gesetz befahl.

Our fate has been weighed
on the hairfine scales of Job,
as desolate as on Doomsday,
we are known heart and soul.

Endless court proceedings
mirror the image of our plight.
No one knows the way completely,
Each stretch of it strikes us blind.

No one can profit from redemption,
this star lies too high to grasp,
should you reach your destination,
you'd still be blocking your path.

Offered up to powers
over which we have lost our sway,
no life can here find flower
without first withering away.

From the center of destruction
now and then a ray may break,
but none shows the direction
the Law commanded us to take.

Seit dies trauervolle Wissen
unantastbar vor uns steht,
ist ein Schleier jäh zerrissen,
Gott, vor deiner Majestät.

Dein Prozeß begann auf Erden;
Endet er vor deinem Thron?
Du kannst nicht verteidigt werden,
hier gilt keine Illusion.

Wer ist hier der Angeklagte?
Du oder die Kreatur?
Wenn dich einer drum befragte,
du versänkst in Schweigen nur.

Kann solch Frage sich erheben?
Ist die Antwort unbestimmt?
Ach, wir müssen dennoch leben,
bis uns dein Gericht vernimmt.

Now that this melancholy knowledge
stands before us, out of reach,
a veil has suddenly been rent,
Lord, before your majesty.

Your trial began on earth;
will it end before your throne?
You cannot be defended,
no illusion here will hold.

Who here stands accused?
Mankind? Or is it you?
Should anyone dare inquire,
you would just stand mute.

Can such a question be raised?
Is the answer in dispute?
Ah, we must live on all the same
until called to witness by your court.

BIALIK

Er war so mitteilsam, daß seine Rede
fast anonym in ihrer Größe blieb.
Er lebte so ins Volk hinein, daß jede
Begegnung ihn zu tieferm Ausdruck trieb.

Sein Tod ist nur die Pause im Gespräche,
in der er tief versunken an sich halt—
Ach, wer doch dies verwünschte Schweigen bräche,
das ihn entrückt und uns im Ohre gellt.

17 Juli 1934

BIALIK

So communicative was he that his words
were almost anonymous in their reach.
So close was he to the people's world
that each encounter deepened his speech.

His death is but a pause in the conversation
in which, lost in thought, he still perseveres—
Ah, who could break this cursèd silence,
which carries him off, screaming in our ears.

17 July, 1934

VAE VICTIS—ODER DER TOD IN DER PROFESSUR

In die alten Bücher ging ich hinein—
Mich dünkten die Zeichen groß.
Ich blieb zu lange mit ihnen allein,
Ich konnte nicht mehr los.

Die Wahrheit hat den alten Glanz,
Doch das Unglück stellt sich ein:
Das Band der Geschlechter bindet nicht ganz,
Das Wissen ist nicht rein.

Verworrnes Gesicht von der Fülle der Zeit
Habe ich heimgebracht.
Ich war zum Sprung auf den Grund bereit,
Aber habe ich ihn gemacht?

Die Symbole der Väter sind hier formuliert;
Der Kabbalist war kein Narr.
Doch was die verwandelte Zeit gebiert
Bleibt fremd und unsichtbar.

Die verwandelte Zeit sieht uns grausam an;
Sie will nicht mehr zurück.

VAE VICTIS—OR, DEATH IN PROFESSORIATE

I threw myself into ancient books.
I was awestruck by their signs.
I spent too much time alone with them.
I could no longer leave them behind.

The glimmer of Truth is ancient,
Yet disaster is unforeseen:
Generations are weakly linked,
And knowledge is not clean.

I have brought back the blurred face
Of the fullness of time.
I was ready to leap into the abyss,
But did I dare to make it mine?

The ancestral symbols are here explained;
The Kabbalist was no dope.
But what time transformed here proposes
Remains foreign, beyond our scope.

Time transformed casts us a fearsome glance,
For it is unwilling to turn back again.

Die Vision der Erlösung in Qualen zerrann.
Was bleibt, ist verworfenes Glück.

Hans Jonas, dem gnostischen
Kollegen,
zur Beherzigung beim Abstieg
in die Tiefen des Nichts
und beim Aufstieg ins noch
Unbekanntere
freundschaftlich eröffnet
von Gerhard Scholem
1943

Gone, the vision of salvation through pain,
What remains, the luck we tossed away.

> *To Hans Jones, my gnostic colleague,*
> *on the occasion of his descent*
> *into the depths of the void*
> *and his reascent into the greater*
> *unknown*
> *offered in friendship*
> *by Gerhard Scholem*
> *1943*

DIE SIRENEN

Manchen Tag, wenn du dein Leben schon
wieder sahst in ruhigen Bahnen rinnen,
hörst du sie mit tiefem Klageton
ihren unverhofften Ruf beginnen,

der, noch ehe er aufs Höchste schwoll,
schon daherbraust wie ein wilder Föhn;
und im Nu sind alle Straßen voll
von dem unerbittlichen Gestöhn,

dessen langgezognes Auf und Ab
dich auf hohen Wogen von Entsetzen
steil hinaufträgt und dann tief hinab
bis er deine Seele dir in Fetzen

reißt. Dann aber bricht die Stille aus,
die in sich den Nachhall jener schrillen
Töne trägt und nimmt dir deinen Willen,
der gelähmt ist durch den stummen Graus.

Mit dem Schweigen halten sie dich fest,
so als schlügen sie auf dich mit Keulen,
bis ein letztes monotones Heulen
endlich dich aus ihrem Bann entläßt.

Sept. 47

THE SIRENS

There are days when seeing your life
resume its normal placid course,
you hear their unexpected cry
arise in lamentation, deep and hoarse,

which, before reaching its highest pitch,
gusts forth like a wild spring wind;
and suddenly all the streets are thick
with the endless sound of groans

whose unrelenting ups and downs
heave you high onto steep waves
of terror, then plunge you to the ground
until your soul, torn apart, caves

in. But then all the silence
within the echo of these shrieks
erupts, and your will goes weak,
stunned by the horror of such stillness.

Falling mute, they reduce you to a cower,
As if covering you with blows,
Until one final monotonous moan
at last releases you from their power.

Sept. 47

JERUSALEM
(SOMMER 1948)

Wenn sich nachts aus heißen Sandsteinmauern
die am Tage absorbierte Glut
in die sommermüde Stadt vertut
und dorthin, wo die Gewehre lauern,

und das kalte Mondlicht die Konturen
ferner Berge formt am Horizont,
während Glockenschlag von Klosteruhren,
sich vermischt mit Schüssen von der Front,

spürst du, daß das säkulare Leben
dieser Stadt mit Macht zuende rinnt,
und du weißt: sie hat sich ausgegeben
im Realen, und beginnt

von der Gegenwart sich abzulösen.
Arm entthront und kahl in ihrer Blöße
Steht sie da, die Feinden nicht erlag,

und ist wieder, was sie längst gewesen:
nur Erinnerung an alte Größe
und ein Warten auf den letzten Tag.

JERUSALEM
(SUMMER 1948)

Nights, when the sandstone walls, baked
all day, now release their gathered heat
onto the city's fitful summer sleep,
wafting up to where weapons lie in wait,

and where the cool moonlight scours
the distant contours of the mountains,
while bells ring from monastery towers,
chiming in on gunfire from the front,

you sense that all the age-old life pent
up in this city now draws to an end,
and you know: she is now spent,
expended on the Real, and commences

to detach herself from the present.
Poor, dethroned, stark in her nakedness,
she stands there, whom enemies could not sway,

and is once again what she always was:
a mere memory of a former greatness
and a waiting for the Final Day.

AN FRAU EVA EHRENBERG

Replik auf ihre Antwort
an Herrn Gerschom Scholem
auf seinen Brief "Wider den
Mythos vom deutsch—jüdischen
Gespräch"

Sehr verehrte gnädige Frau!
Leider weiß ich sehr genau,
was sich einst in Deutschland tat,
weiß auch: manchen, die's betrifft,
scheint die bitter Wahrheit Gift.

Daß Sie lieber desperat
sich am Selbstbetrug berauschen,
ist kein neues Phänomen,
das mich zwänge aufzulauschen.
Hab' das schon in jungen Jahren
allzunah um mich erfahren,
kann's nur allzu gut verstehn.

Ehre Ihren Illusionen
die im leeren Raume wohnen!
Doch bekenne ich sehr gern:
Meinem Sinn liegt gänzlich fern,

TO MRS. EVA EHRENBERG

Reply to her answer to
Mr. Gershom Scholem's letter
"Against the Myth of
German-Jewish Dialogue"

My dear lady, most esteemed,
I alas know too well indeed
of past events in Germany,
and know: those who suffered them
see the bitter truth as poison.

That you should choose
the drug of self-delusion
comes as no surprise
nor does it open my eyes.
I saw case after case
of this in my early days
and understand it all too well.

Honor your illusions,
castles in the air!
Yet of this I am quite aware:
far from me to be so ashamed
of the awful truth

trauriger Wahrheit mich zu schämen,
sie mit Pathos zu verbrämen.

Meine Wahrheit, ohne Glanz,
weiht dem unseligen Popanz
der deutsch—jüdischen Allianz,
den Sie so beredt beweinen,
kein Begräbnis erster Klasse,

Boshaft will ich nicht erscheinen,
doch, fürwahr, ich überlasse
neidlos Ihnen diesen Kranz,
den Sie dem Gespräche flochten,
das wir nie zu hören vermochten.

Los Angeles,
Den 19. September 1965

as to wrap it in the name
of pathos or commiseration.

My truth, without adulteration,
refuses to mourn
this scarecrow on a broom
of the German-Jewish Alliance
which you so eloquently bemoan:
let it go to its doom,
buried without honors.

I do not want to seem crude,
but I leave it entirely up to you
to lay the wreath you have woven
for all the speeches so dear
we could never bear to hear.

Los Angeles,
19 September 1965

AN INGEBORG BACHMANN
nach ihrem Besuch im Ghetto von Rom

Im Ghetto sahst du, was nicht jeder sieht
und was sich draußen allzu leicht vergißt:
Daß nichts ganz voll erfüllt ist, was geschieht,
daß noch nicht aller Tage Abend ist.

Es ist die älteste von alten Kunden,
von denen wir bei den Propheten lesen.
Sie ist uns Juden niemals ganz entschwunden,
doch ist der Preis dafür zu hoch gewesen.

Wir lebten in den Ritzen der Geschichte:
Was nie sich ganz schließt, hat uns Schutz gewährt.
Dem letzten Tage galten die Gesichte,
von denen wir uns im Exil genährt.

Denn alle Tage haben einen Abend.
Doch sollte dereinst alles anders sein:
Der letzte Abend, uns mit Trost erlabend,
sammelt die Strahlen der Erlösung ein.

So sprach zu uns der Geist der Utopie,
in der sich Trost und Unglück dunkel einen.

TO INGEBORG BACHMANN
After her visit to the ghetto of Rome

In the ghetto you saw what few can see
and what memory too easily mislays:
That nothing that happens is entirely fulfilled,
that evening has not yet fallen on all the days.

It is the oldest of those ancient tidings
which we read in the prophets' words.
We Jews have always remembered this news,
though the price we paid has been absurd.

We have existed in the rifts of history,
taking shelter in what is never quite closed.
The final day was the focus of those visions
from which in exile we drew our hopes.

For all days have an evening in the end.
Yet there was a promise of exemption:
The final evening, soothing us, consoling us,
ingathering all the rays of redemption.

So the spirit of Utopia spoke to us,
where consolation darkly joins with fear.

Statt ihrer blieb uns nur Melancholie,
und alles was von Trost blieb, war das Weinen.

Wir können niemals ganz nach Hause kommen.
Die Boten Zions reden uns vom Glück.
Doch haben wir's einmal vorweggenommen,
der Ruf zur Heimkehr gibt es nicht zurück.

Die Botschaft rief zur Heimkehr uns hinüber.
Sie hat das Ghetto viel zu spät erreicht.
Die Stunde der Erlösung ist vorüber,
der Untergang am letzten Abend—leicht.

4. Februar 1967

But instead we fell into melancholy,
finding solace only in our tears.

Zion's messengers speak to us of elation,
but we can never quite return back home.
Though we were once filled with anticipation,
this call to to home can't be restored.

The message that called us home
reached the ghetto far too late.
The hour of redemption is over,
the final day's decline—too plain.

4 February 1967

NOTES TO THE INTRODUCTION

Over your inconsistency: The poem in question begins: "*Die Söhne des Glückes beneid ich nicht....*" A full translation of the poem can be found in *The Complete Poems of Heinrich Heine: A Modern English Version* by Hal Draper (Boston: Suhrkamp/Insel, 1982).

"Papa worked on Yom Kippur": See Scholem, *From Berlin to Jerusalem: Memories of My Youth* (New York: Schocken Books, 1980).

the blessing: from Scholem's 1978 essay, "*Zur Sozialpsychologie der Juden in Deutschland 1900–1930.*"

hundreds of pages from those days: Scholem's notebooks have been edited in two volumes by K. Gründer, H. Kopp-Oberstebrink, and F. Niewöhner, *Gershom Scholem. Tagebücher, nebst, Aufsätzen und Entwürfen bis 1923.* Erster Hallband: 1913-1917. Zweiter Hallband: 1917-1923 (Frankfurt am Main: Jüdischer Verlag im Suhrkamp Verlag, 1995/2000). A selection of these has been translated by Anthony David Skinner as *Lamentations of Youth: The Diaries of Gershom 1913-1919* (Cambridge: Harvard University Press, 2007).

Cynthia Ozick: "The Fourth Sparrow: The Magesterial Reach of Gershom Scholem,' in *Art & Ardor* (New York: Alfred A. Knopf, 1983).

"degeneracy" and "impotent hallucination": Gershom Scholem, *On the Possibility of Jewish Mysticism in Our Time & Other Essays* (Philadelphia and Jerusalem: The Jewish Publication Society, 1997).

"Alchemie und Kabbalah": In *Alchemistische Blätter: Monatszeitschrift für das Gesamtgebiet der Hermetischen Wissenschaften in alter und neuer*

98

Zeit, Organ verschiedener Alcheimisticher Gessellschaften, Logen, Schulen.
This long-forgotten publication was rediscovered by Hans Thomas
Hakl, who suggests that it indicates Scholem's "personal interest in
mystico-occult movements."

—

Moses as a model: from Scholem's diaries: "When Moses was roam-
ing about in solitary mountan deserts to seek God, he heard a voice
saying: 'Put off thy shoes from off thy feet, for the place whereon thou
standest is holy ground.'...You who seek God on your lonely paths,
hear this saying....Remember that God can meet you wherever you
seek Him." For his comments on Herzl, see the notes to the first poem
in this collection.

"identification" and "distance": Scholem used these terms in his vale-
dictory address at Eranos, published in the *Eranos-Jahrbuch*, 1979.

Jeremy Adler: "There Stood My Mr. Benjamin," *Times Literary
Supplement*, June 7, 1996 Scholem's 1915 revelation should be compared
to the inverse transformation of Franz Rosenzweig who, on the Day
of Atonement in 1913, experienced his famous *metanoia*, returning to
Judaism after teetering on the brink of conversion to Christianity.

For more on Scholem's self-aggrandizement and sense of himself as
a messiah figure see Michael Brenner's "From Self-Declared Messiah to
Scholar of Messianism: The Recently Published Diaries Present Young
Gershom Scholem in a New Light," *Jewish Social Studies* (1996). For
example, from a notebook entry dated May 22, 1915: "And the young man
went alone through the world and looked around for where the soul of
his people waited for him. For he was deeply convinced that the soul of
Judah went astray among the nations and waited in the Holy Land for

the one who holds himself impudent enough to liberate her from exile and separation from her people. And he knew deep in his heart that he was the Chosen One, the one to seek and to find his people's soul. And the Dreamer—his name already marked him as the Awaited One: Scholem, the perfect one [Hebrew, *shalem*—complete, perfect] prepared himself for his task and began to forge the weapons of knowledge."

—

"*Two Poems by Friedrich Hölderin*": in *Walter Benjamin: Selected Writings, Volume I* (Cambridge: The Belknap Press, *1996*) The essay (translated by Stanley Corngold) was written in 1914-15, but was not published during Benjamin's lifetime.

"*Lyric of the Kabbalah?*": *Der Jude 6* (1921-1922).

—

PILEGESCH: A small circle of Scholem's friends began to gather in the thirties, usually on Sabbath afternoons, at Lichtheim's home. All were of German background, but they were from diverse scholarly disciplines.

Hans J. Polotsky: Orientalist and linguist of extraordinary range, whose work took him to Greek, Coptic, Syriac, Arabic, Turkish and Iranian dialects, Ethiopic languages, Russian, and numerous European languages.

Hans Jonas: see note to "Vae Victis."

George Lichtheim: Berlin-born historian, political scientist, and foreign editor of the *Jerusalem Post*. Later, London editor of *Commentary*. A close friend and translator of Scholem.

Schmuel Sambursky: Scientist and historian; he wrote on the physical world of the Greeks, Stoics, and Late Antiquity. Noted for his humor.

eulogy for Lewy: Lewy died in 1945.

Nicht-imaginäre Portraits: Non-imaginary portraits.

Knittelverse: Akin to English Skeltonics.

letter to Salman Schocken: "A Candid Letter about My True Intentions in Studying Kabbalah" (1937), in *On the Possibility of Jewish Mysticism*.

———

Scholem called it the abyss: Steven E. Ashheim, *Scholem, Arendt, Klemperer: Intimate Chronicles in Turbulent Times* (Bloomington and Indianapolis: Indiana University Press, 2001) speaks of "Scholem's penchant for the demonic, his early and enduring intuition of what he called the 'abyss,' his fascination with the nihilistic impulse." See also "Thoughts about Our Language," in *On the Possibility of Jewish Mysticism*: "What will be the result of updating the Hebrew language? Is not the holy language, which we have planted among our children, an abyss that must open up?... We live with this language as on the edge of an abyss, yet nearly all of us walk there with confidence, like blind men."

———

Jean Paul: the pseudonym of Johann Paul Friedrich Richter (1763-1825), German fantasist whose work has been compared to Laurence Sterne's and which was translated into English by Carlyle.

Goethe: "The truth that long ago was found, / Has all noble spirits bound, / The ancient truth, take hold of it"—which sums up Scholem's essay "Revelation and Tradition as Religious Categories in Judaism," originally delivered as a lecture at Eranos in 1962, published in *The Messianic Idea in Judaism* (New York: Schocken Books, 1971). Likewise in "My Way to Kabbalah," his acceptance speech for the Bavarian Academy of Arts Literary Prize, he quotes Goethe's *Faust* in the context of describing his own relation to Hebrew: "Over the course of twelve years 'I studied it diligently, with warm effort.'"

his 1930 tribute to… Rosenzweig: See Paul Mendes-Flohr's *The Philosophy of Franz Rosenzweig* (Waltham: Brandeis University Press, 1988).

the Buber-Rosenzweig Bible translation: See *The Messianic Idea in Judaism*. Scholem closes his remarks with a quietly complicated comment on the position of German in the lives of those who would read the Buber-Rosenzweig version, certainly alluding to circles of Jewish scholarship: "As to what the Germans will do with your translation, who can venture to say? For more has happened to the Germans than Hölderlin foresaw when he said: 'it is not ill if certain things be lost, / and living sound from discourse fade away.' For many of us the living sound which you tried to evoke in the German language has faded away. Will anyone be found to take it up again?"

———

a late speech: upon accepting the literary prize from the Bavarian Academy in 1974.

———

he translated… kinot: *In Walter Benjamin: Story of a Friendship* (New York: New York Review of Books, 2003), Scholem writes: "In those days I also translated quite a bit of medieval religious poetry; I read these translations to [Benjamin] and he encouraged me to publish some of them. In connection with our numerous conversations about laments and lamentations he was particularly taken with my translation of a famous medieval lamentation about the burning of the Talmud at Paris in 1240, a rendition which I had made under the influence of Hölderlin's translations." The Scholem archives at the Jewish National and University Library list some fourteen biblical and medieval kinot that he translated, in addition to six other biblical translations and nine other medieval hymns. See also Scholems' *On Jews & Judaism*: "I wanted to write on the Book of Lamentations and the *kinot* as a literary genre. I had a metaphysical theory on the essence of the *kinot*. At that time I wrote a number of things which I have never published: a commentary on the Book of Jonah, another one on Job—or rather, a basis for a commentary on Jonah and Job—metaphysical reflections of mine that were suppressed."

———

his Trauerspiel... *thesis*: *Ursprung des deutschen Trauerspiels* [*The Origin of German Tragic Drama*] (Berlin: E. Rowohlt, 1928).

———

he said that Adorno: in a letter to Hannah Arendt, August 6, 1945.
Buber... "poetry": Scholem called Buber's work "poetry" in a conversation with Richard Kostelanetz (*Present Tense*, 1977).

———

George Mosse: Berlin-born U. S. historian whose later books include *The Crisis of German Ideology* (1964), *Nazi Culture* (1966), and *Germans and Jews* (1968).

"woe to the Volk ... ": drawn from diary entry for November 26, 1914. Aschheim describes *Bildung* as "that middle-class, gradualist, meliorist, inward doctrine of self-cultivation and bourgeois respectability."

———

The bestowal upon him of the Bialik Prize: For the English translation of Scholem's acceptance speech see "Understanding the Internal Processes," in his *On the Possibility of Jewish Mysticism*.

Bialik's essay: Scholem's translation appeared in *Der Jude 4* (1919-1920). English translations of both "*Halachah* and *Aggadah*" (translated by Leon Simon) and "Revealment and Concealment in Language" (translated by Jacob Sloan) appear in *Revealment and Concealment: Five Essays* by Haim Nahman Bialik (Jerusalem: Ibis Editions, 2000).

———

the literary prize from the Bavarian Academy: An English translation of Scholem's acceptance speech entitled "My Way to Kabbalah" appears in *On the Possibility of Jewish Mysticism*.

Reinhold in *A Life of Letters* (Cambridge: Harvard University Press, 2002): "The difference couldn't have been greater between Gershom and the old *Deutschnationaler*, as Reinhold continued to define himself. Yet Reinhold proved one of his brother's best critics. He rightly saw that within his brother—the ardent Zionist and famous scholar of Judaism—was a writer, biographer, and memoirist, a product of European civilization" (*A Life in Letters*).

"I don't know anything about your worldwide status": February 29, 1972.

"Paradox is a characteristic of truth": epigraph to *Sabbatai Sevi: The*

Mystical Messiah, by Gershom Scholem (Princeton: Princeton University Press, 1973).

———

Jews who created the cult of Goethe: see Paul Mendes-Flohr, *German Jews: A Dual Identity* (New Haven: Yale University Press, 1999). For instance: "It is only through the study of Goethe, Benjamin explained, that the nature of Jewishness is fully revealed." And Scholem himself wrote: "Almost all the most important critical interpretations of Goethe were written by Jews!"

———

"All in all … I find myself": from a letter to Harry Heymann, November 12, 1916.

"enigmatic anarchism": in Adler, in the *TLS*.

"the fatal 'modern' conflation": *A Life in Letters*.

Lehre: here the term refers to Torah.

"his disillusion led to despair": Adler, in the *TLS*.

Brit Shalom: "An organization founded in the mid-1920s by Arthur Ruppin and a group of university intellectuals (in which Magnes, Hugo Bergmann, Buber were also active). Brit Shalom called for a binational state with equal rights for Arabs and Jews, and in contrast to the 'political Zionists' of left and right (Ben Gurion and Jabotinsky, respectively it prophetically foresaw that a perpetual conflict between Arabs and Jews would threaten Zionism itself'" (Anson Rabinbach, in his introduction to *The Correspondence of Walter Benjamin and Gershom Scholem* (New York: Schocken Books, 1989). "Bergmann called their group 'the last flicker of the humanist nationalist flame, at a historical moment when nationalism became, among the nations, an antihumanist movement'" (*A Life in Letters*). In the 1977 interview, "The Mystic's Medium," Scholem admits that later in life he came to consider Brit Shalom's political position naïve: "It has come out that almost all dual-national countries explode from within. Forces tear them asunder. I don't say I'm glad about this; history shows this." Elsewhere Scholem has said that the question of whether Brit Shalom was right or wrong in its approach "has never been crucial"; instead, he says of Brit Shalom, "for me it was a symbol of conduct" (*On Jews & Judaism*).

"fatal attraction to messianism": in "The Threat of Messianism: An interview with Gershom Scholem," *The New York Review of Books* (1980), Scholem explains to David Biale the development of his political views in the wake of World War II and the various attempts at rapprochement with Israel's Arab neighbors. Here he returns to his early and deep-seated suspicion of the fusion of religion and politics: "Today we have the Gush Emunim which is definitely a messianic group. They use biblical verses for political purposes. Whenever messianism is introduced into politics, it becomes a very dangerous business. It can only lead to disaster."

"I believe in the existence of absolute values": from *On the Possibility of Jewish Mysticism.*

"I don't understand atheists": from *On Jews & Judaism.*

---

laudatio *to Buber*: from *The Messianic Idea in Judaism.*

"correspond with equals": A separate volume might be devoted to the poems exchanged in these circles. In 1962 Scholem reminisced that he

still "preciously guards a great poem written [by his cousin Pflaum] in medieval Latin for my 25th birthday."

———

Eulogy for...Lea Goldberg. An English translation of the eulogy (with this title) appeared in the *Jerusalem Post* on January 23, 1970.

he told Irving Howe: from "Irving Howe Interviews Gershom Scholem. The Only Thing in My Life I Have Never Doubted Is the Existence of God," *Present Tense* (1980). The discussion centers on the question of European and modernist influence on Hebrew literature; Howe had mentioned Appelfeld, Amichai, Ravikovich, Oz, Yehoshua, and Yaakov Shabtai, noting that it was to be expected that they "should share tastes, styles, sensibilities with European and American writers."

———

"What the value and worth of language will be": from "The Name of God and the Linguistic Theory of the Kabbala," *Diogenes* (1972).

———

"the master of disenchantment": "The Remembrancer: Rescuing Walter Benjamin from the Acolytes," *Times Literary Supplement* (1993). Steiner wrote about Scholem on several occasions. See "The Friend of a Friend," *The New Yorker* (1990), and "A friendship and Its Flaws," *TLS* (1980), both about the Scholem-Benjamin correspondence. The 1980 article begins: "This must be one of the saddest books in the world."

———

the scholar reflected on his missed opportunities: "The discovery of the tremendous poetic potential within Kabbalah, in its own unique language no less than in its poetry proper...all these constitute a realm which has hardly been examined and which holds the promise of great discoveries....My own secret longing to do so [i.e., to fully encompass the question of this poetic potential] has not been fulfilled and remains unsatisfied." In "Understanding the Internal Processes," *On the Possibility of Jewish Mysticism*.

———

"Judaic" high-culture: In "the Friend of a Friend," *The New Yorker* (1990) George Steiner writes, "Not only have [Scholem's] studies of the Cabala altered, albeit controversially, the image of Judaism—the understanding that even an agnostic Jew now has of his psychological and historical provenance—but his explorations, translations, and presentations of Cabalistic writings exercise a formidable influence on literary theory at large, on the ways in which non-Jewish and wholly agnostic critics and scholars read poetry." This is also the thrust of an essay by the late Israeli critic Yoram Bronowski, "The Impact of Gershom Scholem's Thought on Intellectual Life in Israel," in *The Jewish Quarterly* (1984): "Scholem's influence on an entire generation's approach to Judaism is such that nowadays there is another danger, looming on the intellectual horizon in Israel as well as in Jewish circles abroad, mainly in the USA. A historian of Jewish philosophy, who teaches at an American university, told me once that for most students Judaism is mysticism, and the greatest book of this Judaism is ... *Major Trends in Jewish Mysticism*."

———

Ernst Bloch: see "Does God Dwell in the Heart of an Atheist?", an essay in honor of Bloch's ninetieth birthday in *On the Possibility of Jewish Mysticism*.

Walt Whitman: "Who knows where the boundaries of holiness lie?... Perhaps holiness will be revealed within the innermost sanctums of...secularity, and the traditional concepts fail to recognize mysticism in its new forms?... [T]hose of use who labor here as Jews in the Land of Israel may find great interest in the book of poems by Walt Whitman, who a hundred years ago sang the song of American with a feeling of the absolute sanctity of the absolutely secular." From "Reflections on the Possibility of Jewish Mysticism in Our Time" in *On the Possibility of Jewish Mysticism*. In an interview that appears in *On Jews & Judaism*, he said: "The question is whether in the reality in which today's secular person lives, the [symbolic] dimension will be revealed again. I was strongly criticized when I dared to say that Walt Whitman's writing contain something like this. Walt Whitman revealed in an utterly naturalistic world what Kabbalists and other mystics revealed in their world."

William Blake: "There are things which structurally have some affinity to Kabbalah—decidedly, in my opinion....To a modern man who studies the Kabbalah, Blake's world is very familiar" ("The Mystic's Medium").

———

"the revolution of a language": See "Thoughts about Our Language," in *On the Possibility of Jewish Mysticism*.

Moshe Idel, Kabbalah: New Perspectives (New Haven: Yale University Press, 1988).

the fullness of time: See notes to "Vae Victis—Or, Death in the Professoriate."

NOTES TO THE POEMS

The original German versions of these poems may be found in the Jewish National and University Library, Department of Manuscripts and Archives, Gershom Scholem Archives, Jerusalem, Arc. 4 ° 1599/277-III, "Poems and Limericks." Versions from the notebooks and other sources have also been consulted. Throughout, irregularities of Scholem's punctuation and capitalization have been maintained.

TO THEODOR HERZL

Written at age 17 in his notebook. While the poem is dated 1915, it may in fact have been written a year earlier, to mark the tenth anniversary of Herzl's death. Theodor Herzl (1860-1904) was the founder of the modern Zionist movement. Scholem applied similar language to his own generation in a diary entry of August 17, 1914: "We do not know, but we shall prepare the way for the angel who is coming, so that another Herzl may arise for us, the later-born, one who is whole to guide his hesitant brethren. He provided youth with a hope, old age with a dream, mankind with something beautiful....[W]e bear the myth of Theodor Herzl within ourselves like a sacred fire....Do you want always to let the fire die down to the embers? He left you the flag, and is not the flag an order to begin the march?"

MENASHE CHAYIM

The Hebrew *menashe chayim* means, literally, "who makes life forget." This is the second of two sonnets Scholem wrote under this title. The first is dated 1918, the second undated. A Hebrew translation of the poem by Scholem himself is dated Passover, 1919. There is an epigraph that appears to apply to both parts of the poem and reads: "*Nur Leid ist Größe und noch keiner fand / ohne dies Wissen in das heilge Land*" ("Only sorrow is greatness and without it / no one has yet found knowledge in the Holy Land").

Elsewhere Scholem writes: "Agnon...was no intellectual but rather a man from the world of creativity in which the fountains of imagination bubbled most richly. His conversations had a thoroughly profane character and content, but he spoke in the style of the heroes of his stories, and there was something infinitely attractive about his manner of speaking. I gave expression to my admiration for him in two sonnets which I wrote in German in praise of Menashe Chayim, the hero of *And the Crooked Shall Be Made Straight*....I sent them to Agnon and thereby earned a place in his heart—evidently I was the first to write poems about his books." Scholem also translated several Agnon stories into German for the magazine *Der Jude*.

PARAPHRASE, FROM THE PROSE OF "THE DIARY"

"The Diary" mentioned in the title of this poem is a section of Benjamin's "The Metaphysics of Youth," from Walter Benjamin, *Selected Writings*, Volume I. Written in 1913-1914, the essay was unpublished in Benjamin's lifetime. Scholem copied the essay out longhand when Benjamin gave it to him, and he responds to Benjamin's work in this poem. Scholem later referred to the "genius" of Benjamin's essay which begins: "We wish to pay heed to the sources of the unnameable despair that flows in every soul. The souls listen expectantly to the melody of their youth....One day they awake to despair: the first day of the diary."

While he was in Muri and intensively reading poetry with Benjamin, Scholem experienced an outpouring of verse. Between May 12 and 15 he wrote at least ten poems. This poem is one of seven—in a series he titled "Seven Sonnets to Three Women Friends," i.e., Meta Jahr, Grete Brauer, and Dora Benjamin—that Scholem appended to a letter he sent to Jahr, a friend from Berlin, in late May of 1918.

In the gathering of sonnets the poem was initially entitled "Farewell to a Young Girl V." The Belovèd of line 7 is Grete Brauer, to whom Scholem confessed in a letter of March 7, 1918, that she was, with Walter Benjamin, the "midpoint" of his life. In its original version, the last two lines of the poem ran: "The present shall disunite us before God / Me and the diary that shouts forth from you."

FAREWELL TO A YOUNG GIRL

One of the "Seven Sonnets to Three Women Friends," entitled "Farewell to a Young Girl II" in the archive autograph version. This poem, too, is addressed to Grete Brauer, who had recently rejected Scholem. In Scholem's impassioned letter from Jena of March 7, 1918, the composition of which he says "precipitated a crisis that will either bring perfect purity to my life or shatter it to pieces," he had told her that it was "the pure power of her *Dasein*" that had kept him "healthy" and that had prevented him from "being consumed" in the "furnace" in which he was then living. The "lament" of line 1 most likely alludes to the Hebrew Book of Lamentations, which Scholem had been translating, as well as to his essay on "Lament and Lamentation" and the medieval *kinot* that had preoccupied him for quite some time. "You'll grasp the deepest meaning of the Lamentations," he writes to Grete, "when you read them as a *confession* of my state—as it no doubt is." Itta Shedletzky points out the central role the biblical and medieval lamentations played in the development of Scholem's Judaism—wherein he had to mourn the religion of the past, which had been lost to emancipation and assimilation, in order for him to proceed with his mission of renewal. In this poem the various forms of "*Unglück*" or "misfortune" affecting his life at the time crystallize around his lamented relationship with Grete and become the guarantor of his dream of Zion.

FOR JULY 15

Scholem writes of the centrality for Benjamin of what he calls in this poem "the promise of Teaching," noting that Benjamin was then preoccupied with the "religious sphere," and that *Lehre* (teaching) "for him included the philosophical realm that definitely transcended it. In his early writings he reverted repeatedly to this concept, which he interpreted in the sense of the original meaning of the Hebrew *torah* as 'instruction,' instruction not only about the true condition and way of man in the world but also about the transcausal connection of things and their rootedness in God." Scholem adds that his friend had "no compunctions about speaking undisguisedly of God. Since we both believed in God, we never discussed His 'existence.'" The autograph copy in the archive is clearly dated 15.5.1918, as is "The Ball," which is copied out on the back of the same small piece of paper. It appears that Scholem wrote this poem, in anticipation of his friend's July birthday, during his mid-May wave of inspiration. It is also possible, however, that the date in Scholem's hand involves a slip on his part, and that in fact both were written in July.

THE BALL

"The Ball" treats another section of Benjamin's essay "The Metaphysics of Youth." Written just three days after "Paraphrase, from the Prose of 'The Diary,'" this poem continues the response that Scholem began there. This section of Benjamin's essay describes a dream ball, one of the "invisible dreams" we "carry around with us" in our youth: "The music…transports our thoughts; our eyes reflect our friends around us, how they all move, surrounded by the flowing night. We are truly in a house without windows, a ballroom without world….We know that all the merciless realities that have been expelled still flutter round this house. The poets with their bitter smiles, the saints and the policemen, and the waiting cars. From time to time, music penetrates to the outside world and submerges them."

W. B.

Sonnet presented to Benjamin on his on his birthday, July 15, 1918. Summing up his bond with Benjamin in *Story of a Friendship*, Scholem quotes his own diary entry from November 9, 1918, and mentions this poem: "After a half-year of being together our relationship—the most decisive one of my life (with a man, at any rate)—appears in a clearer light to me. I am sure I have written a lot of nonsense about it in these pages, and in essence that is all wrong—simply because one only can keep silent about it. My sonnet for Benjamin's birthday was my only foray into language. I am beginning to grow inexpressibly fond of Dora again." Dora was Benjamin's wife.

GREETINGS FROM ANGELUS

Sent to Benjamin on the latter's birthday in 1921, this is Scholem's only well-known poem. For the full context, see Scholem's lengthy essay, "Walter Benjamin and His Angel" (in *On Jews & Judaism*). Benjamin thanked Scholem in a letter of July 25, 1921, and on November 8 of that year, reciprocated with a poem of his own. After Scholem had sent him another copy of the poem in a letter the previous month, on October 16, 1933, Benjamin wrote to Scholem: "I read your poem on the *Angelus Novus* again with undiminished admiration. I would place it among the best that I know." Robert Alter notes in *Necessary Angels* that "In 1921 Benjamin acquired Paul Klee's *Angelus Novus*, an oil painting colored with aquarelle executed the previous year. For the rest of his life Benjamin kept the drawing, according to Scholem's testimony, as a kind of spiritual talisman and focus for meditation. Benjamin willed the drawing to Scholem, and it hung in the living room of the Scholem home on Abarbanel Street in Jerusalem until 1989, when it was placed by his widow in the Israel Museum." *Angelus Novus* also inspired the title of a literary journal Benjamin hoped to found in 1921 and in which he planned to publish his essay "The Task of the Translator" as well as poems by Heinle.

MOURNFUL REDEMPTION

Written in 1926, three years after Scholem's arrival in Jerusalem. This was also the year in which Scholem published his first statement in the context of Brit Shalom. That statement, in the *Jüdische Rundschau*, was "directed against the creation of a Jewish Legion and against those who prefer security based on violence to the creation of understanding between human beings." The poem clearly reflects Scholem's engagement with Kabbalah. In his characteristically paradoxical fashion, the occlusion of the light of Zion—in this case a spiritual light—results in nearness to the divine. The echoes of the doctrine of *tzimtzum* (self-contraction) and the shattering of the vessels are conspicuous, as is the shadow of Benjamin's preoccupation with *Trauer*.

THE OFFICIAL ABECEDARIUM

In 1918, after having been declared permanently unfit for army duty (he took pains to be disqualified on psychological grounds), Scholem traveled to Switzerland, where Benjamin was doing his doctorate at Bern. Benjamin and Dora convinced Scholem to take a room in a nearby village, only a two-minute walk from their apartment. There, in Muri, they founded an imaginary institution: "Since so little was to be learned at the university, we formed 'our own academy' (as Benjamin put it in our first conversations). Thus we proceeded to found, half in earnest and half in jest, the 'University of Muri' and its 'institutes': a library and an academy. In the catalogue of this university, the statutes of the academy, and the imaginary list of new library acquisitions, for which Benjamin supplied reviews sparkling with wit, our high spirits and ridicule of academic activities found an appropriate outlet during the next three or four years. Benjamin played the role of the rector....I was heard from as 'Beadle of the School of the Philosophy of Religion'" (*Story of a Friendship*).

Although first published in 1927 in a limited edition chapbook of 250 copies, which was printed by Scholem's brothers, the first version of this poem was presented to Benjamin on his birthday on July 15, 1918.

Translator Richard Sieburth comments: "The abecedarium (whose alphabetical form playfully imitates the lettristic declensions of the

Kabbalists) can be juxtaposed with the activities of Tristan Tzara and his Dada cohorts at the Café Voltaire in Zurich, ca. 1917-1919. Like them, Scholem proposes, via the corrosive effects of doggerel, a kind of tabula rasa of Western philosophy, especially as embodied by its current luminaries in the German academy—from which the young renegades Scholem and Benjamin felt themselves excluded."

Benjamin called "The Abecedarium" the poem to the "guardian angel of the university. . . ."

ENCOUNTER WITH ZION AND THE WORLD

Scholem returns here to the theme of "senselessness" that he addressed in "Greetings from Angelus." A letter to Martin Buber sent a month earlier (May 22, 1930) places this poem in context. "There would be no use in denying that the countenance of the Zionist cause has darkened in catastrophic fashion for us (and by this I mean the people who at bottom are alone in bearing the Brit Shalom). After all, the gloomy insights that we have had do not extend to the political question of the Arabs but concern the physiognomy of a cause that in a historic hour is of necessity assuming definite form—and to have devoted a life to this cause threatens to prove to have been a dubious undertaking. The torment of this condition … is reaching the limits of endurability. After all, we have to realize that our interpretation of Zionism does no good if someday (and there is no mistaking the fact that the decisive hour has come) the face of Zionism, even that which is only turned inward, should prove to be that of a Medusa."

In a 2002 *Ha'aretz* article on Scholem's notebooks, Henry Wasserman writes of the way in which Scholem's "total devotion to Zionism" led to his being "able to criticize Zionism with a harshness that has been displayed by only very few of the movement's critics." Wasserman goes on to quote a 1918 notebook entry by Scholem: "In order to be able to live in Zion, perhaps I will have to be a thoroughly miserable person. I see the sad and extremely depressing options that will emerge in the future."

TO ME OR HER?

The meaning of the title to this poem is obscure. For "the visible loses its power / when times turn more inward" compare Scholem's letter to Buber: "the face of Zionism...which is only turned inward." For the "lie of identity" compare Benjamin's 1916 "Theses on the Problem of Identity" (unpublished in Benjamin's lifetime), in Benjamin's *Selected Writings, Volume I.*

MEDIA IN VITA

This stark confession contains an unmistakable rejection of religious and political consolations. While only a full study of this period of Scholem's biography would yield a dependable answer, it seems certain that he was discouraged by current events, particularly the bloody Arab riots of 1929 and the actions of his fellow Zionists. Typically, his response was not political but rather a thickly overdetermined conflation of history, philology, and mysticism, poured into the crucible of his scholarship—and the rare poem. Some observers see in this "inner exile" from Zionism Scholem's version of Kabbalistic *tzimtzum.*

It is important to note that this is, in a certain sense, the most esoteric of the poems. Not only does the speaker consider putting on a disguise, but he submits to "that abyss / of nothingness in which the world appears." At least one esoteric antecedent for this usage of "abyss" may be noted, and that is in the theosophy of Jakob Boehme. This would seem consistent with the strong impression that Christian Kabbalah more generally made on the young Scholem.

WITH A COPY OF WALTER BENJAMIN'S "ONE-WAY STREET"

Sent to Benjamin in a September 19, 1933 letter, together with a another copy of the 1921 poem "Angelus Novus." "Kitty" is Kitty Steinschneider Marx, life-long friend of Scholem's and Benjamin's, who passed away as this book first went to press in 2003. "One-Way Street," written in 1923–26 and published in 1928, appears in *Benjamin's Selected Writings, Volume 1*.

WITH A COPY OF KAFKA'S TRIAL

The poem, which was written in 1933, was enclosed, with commentary, in Scholem's July 9, 1934, letter to Benjamin: "Some months back, I gave a theological didactic poem on *The Trial* to [Robert] Weltsch, who wanted to print it together with your essay ["Franz Kafka"]. We will present a most pleasant contrast because, as utterly distanced as I feel from the somewhat harmless-idiotic quotations of the 'theological' interpreters you mention, I am still firmly convinced that a theological aspect of this world, in which God does not appear, is the most legitimate of such interpretations." On July 17 he wrote to Benjamin again: "Kafka's world is the world of revelation, but of revelation seen of course from that perspective in which it is returned to its own nothingness.... The *nonfulfillability* of what has been revealed is the point where a *correctly* understood theology (as I, immersed in my Kabbalah, think ...) coincides most perfectly with that which offers the key to Kafka's work." In the earlier letter, Scholem notes that the poem was "composed some time ago for Kitty Marx's theological instruction." (Scholem wrote it out in the copy of *The Trial* that he gave her.) It was published in the *Jüdische Rundschau* in 1935, under the title printed here, but other manuscripts in the archive bear the title "*Lehrgedicht vom 'Prozeß*'" ("A Didactic Poem on *The Trial*"). A note after the poem in the *Jüdische Rundschau* reads: "On the occasion of the publication of the new edition of Kafka's works by Shocken in Berlin. *The Trial* is about to appear as the second volume." The first edition of *The Trial* was published in 1925.

BIALIK

Haim Nahman Bialik (1873-1934), whom Scholem called "our national poet." Skinner comments in *A Life in Letters* that Bialik "admired the twenty-six-year-old for combining so many contradictory talents and passions; he considered Scholem the leading candidate to find 'the lost key to the locked gate of the temple' of Jewish mysticism."

VAE VICTIS

The title means: "Woe to the vanquished."

Hans Jonas (1903-1993), philosopher and scholar of Gnosticism, friend of Scholem and member of PILEGESCH. Scholem wrote this poem into the flyleaf of the copy of the English edition of *Major Trends in Jewish Mysticism* that he presented to Jonas on two different occasions (the circumstances of which are not clear). There are four versions of the poem in the archives: one undated (probably 1941), one dated 1941, one 1942, and one 1943. The version printed here is what Scholem gave Jonas in 1943, when the latter was serving in the Jewish Brigade of the British Army.

There are several variant readings for line 6. In what appears to be the first draft (untitled), the line reads: "*doch wie ihr Künder sein?*" (Yet how to be its herald?). In the 1941 titled autograph copy, the line reads: "*doch wie Empfänger sein?*" (but how are we to receive it?)—implying the Hebrew "*kabbalah*" (literally, reception).

The "fullness of time" was simultaneously a trope for the "end of time" and for a kind of wholeness found within the present—with "end of time" here implying both an end to temporality as such and the arrival at the ultimate. This latter connotation is suggested in Benjamin's contemporaneous notion of the "*Jetztzeit*," the "Now-Time." Some years later Scholem wrote in his poem to Ingeborg Bachmann that "nothing that happens is entirely fulfilled," perhaps thinking of Galatians 4:4 and Ephesians 1:10.

THE SIRENS

While the central literary reference is certainly Kafka's "The Silence of the Sirens," other influences may be noted. These include Heine's "Lorelei" and the discussion of Homer's sirens in Adorno and Horkheimer's *Dialectic of Enlightenment*, which was published in 1947, an annotated copy of which can be found in Scholem's library. As in "Media in Vita," myth (Homer's sirens), philosophy-theology (Kafka, Adorno, and Horkheimer), and history (the literal curfew or ambulance sirens Scholem was no doubt hearing in 1947) are powerfully conflated. Hala Saakini, a Palestinian then-resident of Jerusalem wrote in her memoirs: "With the end of World War II, the long-standing hostility between the Arab population of Palestine and the Zionists flared up again.... Our beautiful Jerusalem became a city of violence and strife....Every few weeks, the city would be shaken by an explosion and immediately the sirens would start wailing, which meant that a curfew was on.... Our American friend Stabler once jokingly described the situation with the words "*zamour, toujours zamour*" (*zamour* being the Arabic word for 'siren')."

JERUSALEM (SUMMER 1948)

Written during Israel's War of Independence. Skinner comments in *A Life in Letters*: "Scholem, an old critic of Ben Gurion and the Labor party, applauded the birth of the State of Israel in May 1948. Yet he never ceased to exercise his right to censure, decrying 'insolent boasting' and 'nationistic phrases.'" Skinner notes in his preface to the letters of the early thirties that, as the stage was being set "for a full scale conflict[,] Scholem warily observed the growth of militancy among his fellow Jews. What disturbed him even more was the place that tradition and the Bible came to play in Jewish nationalism.... In a letter he wrote in 1925 to Rosenzweig, he mockingly described Hebrew's 'spectral degradation' into the Yishuv's 'phantasmagoric Volapük [a kind of Esperanto, Ed.]. Its old messianic powers had vanished, leaving a 'vestigial, ghostly language.'" Scholem's language of the twenties—regarding Zionism—is echoed here in the private poetry of the late forties and the period of Israeli independence.

TO MRS. EVA EHRENBERG

A reply to Eva Ehrenberg's verse epistle to Scholem, dated August 30, 1965, in which she dismisses his letter-essay "Against the Myth of German-Jewish Dialogue" (included in his *On Jews & Judaism*) with the refrain: "There are dialogues that have not died out to this day. / You speak like a blindman speaking of colors." Scholem's letter was written in response to a request from an editor who had asked him to contribute to *Festschrift* that would, among other things, be understood as "a testimony to a German-Jewish dialogue, the core of which is indestructible." Scholem responds: "I deny that there has ever been...a German-Jewish dialogue in any genuine sense whatsoever, i.e., *as a historical phenomenon*. It takes two to have a dialogue...."

TO INGEBORG BACHMANN

Ingeborg Bachmann (1926-1973), Austrian poet, novelist, playwright. This poem was written in response to Bachmann's essay "What I Saw and Heard in Rome" (1955). The key sentence there for Scholem would seem to be: "It is not yet the evening of all days, but on the Day of Atonement everyone is pardoned in advance for an entire year."

—

The last poem Scholem wrote in German was a comic piece of doggerel composed during his recovery from the removal of a kidney-stone in 1972. The manuscript mentioned in the poem is mostly likely his essay, "Walter Benjamin and His Angel," composed on the eightieth anniversary of the latter's birth and which Scholem was planning to send to Germany for publication.

> Huzzah! shouts Scholem's mouth,
> my kidney is again quite sound
> and in this book's four-square space
> the work flows like icing on a cake
> (the whole thing twice revised at this stage).
> Indeed, there is even reason to claim,
> provided the staff here make decent haste,

that within the week to come
my manuscript will be fully done.
Though it is unlikely in my state
it will go beyond the hundredth page.
Kitty and Hedi have typed it alive
for the Suhrkampian archive.
And the author has worked like hell
that the letter of his spirit might excel.
Will you all exclaim: "It's lovely of course!"
when you receive it in the distant North??

TRANSLATOR'S AFTERWORD:
OF ANGELOLOGY AND ADDRESS

To Peter & Adina

In the winter of 2001, a few months after the outset of the Second Intifada, the American scholar Steven Wasserstrom was conducting research at the Gershom Scholem Archive in Jerusalem. Fresh on the heels of the publication of his *Religion After Religion*, a study of three legendary twentieth-century scholars – Mircea Eliade, Henri Corbin, and Gershom Scholem – Wasserstrom was continuing to follow the latter's trail. Among the documents he was exploring in the Jewish and National University Library, he came across a folder labeled "Poems and Limericks." Intrigued, he leafed through the stray sheets, some in Scholem's hand, some in typescript, some previously published in editions of his correspondence or diaries, but the majority of them, so it turned out, as of yet ungathered into a proper German edition – or, for that matter, translated into English.

Around the same time Wasserstrom was meeting with two of his local friends, the writers Peter Cole and Adina Hoffman, who were also co-editors of Ibis Editions, a small, Jerusalem-based English language publishing house devoted to giving a fresh poetical and political valence to the hoary notion of the Levant – that vibrant Mediterranean cultural matrix whose contentious diversities the maverick Zionist Gershom Scholem attempted to negotiate, for better or worse, between his initial emigration to Palestine in 1923 and his wary greeting of foundation of the state of Israel in 1948. As Wasserstrom told them about his finds, they sensed that this largely overlooked material had the makings of an unexpected and revelatory book, and asked him if the poems were strong enough to merit publication. From a historical and scholarly perspective, said Wasserstrom, absolutely. But for an evaluation of their literary quality, someone more versed in German poetry would have to be consulted.

Familiar with my versions of Hölderlin and Benjamin, they turned to me to ask what I thought of the poems, as poems, whether in fact they merited translation and publication, and, if they did, whether I might want to try my hand. As packets of xeroxes began arriving in New York from the Scholem Archive, I spent the spring of 2001 making my way through the manuscripts, trying to see what kind of book – and what kind of English – might emerge from this trove. After much back-and-forthing with Ibis, I eventually arrived at a selection, fully convinced that these were poems worth listening to, especially in translation, written as they were in a German that Scholem always claimed was his second tongue, in comparison to the great originary silence of Biblical Hebrew, his deepest and most private stratum of language. In a 1917 diary entry Scholem observed: "One of the most profound truths of language is how speaking passes from silence to silence, with language lurking between them as the medium of silence. Silence takes place *in* language." Which is to say, it takes place in translation. The challenge, then, when it came to Scholem's verse, was how to convey something of this silence into English. The place I heard it most insistently was, paradoxically, in the poems' actual acts of address: Scholem is always speaking to an absent other, establishing an I-Thou-(We) relationship that seems to escape precise articulation, lying as it does beyond the reach of language – in the realm of angels. This is especially true of the poems directly or indirectly addressed to his closest (and remotest) friend Walter Benjamin – which constitute nearly half the poems I finally chose to include, some of them poems of praise and/or lamentation, others serving as midrashic verse commentaries on the latter's texts.

Scholem never considered his verse compositions to be a major part of his oeuvre: he saw himself first and foremost a scholar. Moreover, he remarks somewhere that he had no interest whatsoever in becoming part of the German literary tradition, except as an author of prose – or as a translator from the Hebrew. But he knew his modern poetry well enough: Benjamin had him read Hölderlin, George, and Rilke, and spoken to him about Baudelaire and Mallarmé. Indeed, it is à propos of Mallarmé that Scholem writes in an early diary entry: "Insight into the art of poetry implies symbolic skepticism about its truth. The theory of poetry is either a stillborn child or the Messiah himself. *There is nothing between!* Poetry is destruction. I'm just a bad poet because I'll never be prepared to give up my life for a poem. I would never risk ruin for a poem." By the absolute standards of his adolescence, Scholem was, by his own account, a "bad poet." Unlike, say, a Celan, none of his poems (except perhaps for those written at a white heat in May, 1918) show him risking existential or linguistic ruin. Indeed, the very fact that he is writing fairly traditional rhymed verse in German keeps him from falling into the abyssal silence of Hebrew (or of a late Hölderlin) and allows him to assume – despite his claim "there is nothing in between" – a middle voice somewhere between the "still-born child" and the "Messiah," somewhere between the active and the passive, pitched for the most to the more prosaic domain of human argument and conversation. And here, seen from a more classical—and less apocalyptic—perspective, he writes poems that, far from being a poetaster's mediocre ventures into verse, are in their own way oddly moving. Scholem is an occasional poet in the most specific sense of the term: his poetry most frequently arises from circumstance, in recognition of a concrete, dialogical juncture or event, whether it be one of Benjamin's birthdays or the ceremonial gift of a book to a friend. The act of dedication or address, he observed of Hölderlin's celebrated poem "To Landauer," was always a form of Revelation, in which the merely occasional or merely private performance of apostrophe promised intimations of deeper disclosure.

As the project now grew in scope, and as Wasserstrom and the Ibis team started working out some sort of apparatus to the volume – which resulted in its fine Introduction and Notes – I spent the summer of 2001 translating Scholem, gradually learning how to overhear his prosopopoeia and to come up with English rhymes and rhythms for his blocky, paratactic quatrains (which respond far better to translation than do his friend Benjamin's clotted sonnets). By 9/11, with the smell of devastation still hanging over the city, I had gotten as far as Scholem's traumatized poems about the violence visited upon Jerusalem in the late 1940s. In 2003, shortly after the outbreak of the Second Gulf War, the volume finally appeared from Ibis Editions under the title *The Fullness of Time*. These poems are, I believe, still actual – particularly in their anguished meditations on the meaning of Zion: "What was within is now without,/ the dream twists into violence,/ and once again we stand outside/ and Zion is without form or sense." I am extraordinarily grateful to Jill Schoolman and Archipelago's archangels for making possible this revised edition of Scholem's verse under the new title *Greetings from Angelus*. Translators are so rarely granted second acts.

———

The first poem that drew me into addressing Scholem was his "Official Didactic Poem of the Faculty of Philosophy of the State University of Muri," an imaginary (counter-) institution of learning that he dreamt up with Walter Benjamin during their draft-dodging days in Switzerland during World War I and that would prove to be a running joke throughout their later correspondence. Published as a limited edition chapbook in 1927 and initially dedicated to Benjamin on his birthday on July 15, 1918, the poem is a Dada (and crypto-kabbalistic) Abecedarium which heaps doggerel derision on the heavyweights of German philosophy:

> D
>
> Nowadays Bergson's Durée
> Elicits nary a hooray.
> Only Dilthey's name, amen,
> Justifies the ways of D to men.

> H
>
> Whatever is modern and ascetic
> Will find Husserl most sympathetic.
> Though there is a rumor going through the land
> He was someone Heidegger could never understand.

> M
>
> Moses ben Maimon meditated the "Moreh."
> The Marburg School caused a great furore.
> Metaphysics and number theory
> Made Ernst Mach extremely leery.

As the couplets fell easily into place, I discovered a puckish, donnish wit, somewhere between Edward Lear, T.S. Eliot and W.H. Auden.

I had never quite realized that behind Scholem's habitual high solemnity as a scholar of religion there lay an antinomian zaniness that he shared with his early idol Benjamin, who at this point in the war was devouring Karl Kraus's satires and Flaubert's great deconstruction of received ideas, *Bouvard and Pécuchet*, while enjoying the various childish parlor (and mind) games he and his wife Dora played at their house in Muri on the outskirts of Bern with their young guest and devotee, Herr Gerhard.

The two young men had first met in 1915 in Berlin, when Scholem was seventeen and a half and Benjamin twenty-three. Scholem would later observe: "From the very outset, Benjamin's markedly courteous manner created a natural sense of distance and seemed to exact reciprocal behavior. This was especially difficult in my case… He was probably the only person toward whom I was almost invariably polite." Proximity at a distance, maintenance of old-fashioned intellectual etiquette in the face of sharp disagreement and latent rivalry – this is the portrait Scholem provides of their ambivalent lifelong relationship in his retrospective *A Story of a Friendship* (1975), in his correspondence, and especially in his private diaries (published in English under the title *Lamentations of Youth* in Anthony David Skinner's translation, from which I extensively quote below). At once too near and too far, too twinned and too estranged, both young men wanted to glimpse in themselves an allegorical mirroring of the other – a better Angel, a spiritual Brother, a Philosopher-Friend – even if, as Scholem admitted, "there often lurked a deep-seated bitterness and disillusionment over the images of one another that we had fashioned for ourselves."

Their earliest discussions focused around the wartime fate of Zionism and the German-Jewish youth movements, on neo-Kantiansm and other philosophic matters – and, significantly enough, on translation.

Benjamin read Scholem examples of his recent versions of Baudelaire and challenged him to distinguish them from those of Stefan George; he declaimed Pindar aloud in the original, accompanied by Hölderlin's visionary renditions of the Greek, which demonstrated just how far one could go in estranging the German language from itself when it came to ancient texts. This in turn led to consideration of new strategies of Bible translation. Scholem, already an accomplished Hebraicist, shared with Benjamin his German accounts of the Song of Songs, later noting in his diaries: "to translate the Bible, a person needs to write it all over again from scratch." Their intense discussions about the philosophy of language (and particularly about the translatability of sacred scripture) bore fruit in Benjamin's 1916 essay "On Language as Such and the Language of Man," – originally addressed as a letter to Scholem and a remarkable document of their early *Symphilosophie*, recording as it did the encounter between Benjamin's studies of the poetic theory of the German romantics and Scholem's growing mastery of the esoteric Jewish tradition of language mysticism. The impress of Scholem's early research into ancient and medieval Hebrew lamentations (*kinot*) can equally be felt in Benjamin's analysis of the work of mourning in the German baroque *Trauerspiel* in two essays he wrote on the topic that same year – preliminary sketches for his major 1928 study, *Ursprung des deutschen Trauerspiels* (*The Origins of German Tragic Drama*). From early on, Benjamin's ventures into this neglected (and proto-modernist) territory of German literary history paralleled Scholem's initial excavations of the Kabbalah, an equally forgotten site of radical Jewish tradition.

According to Scholem's *Story of a Friendship*, Benjamin's "wall of reserve" was buttressed by "a secretiveness bordering on eccentricity, a mystery-mongering that generally prevailed in everything relating to him personally, though it sometimes was breached unexpectedly by private and confidential revelations." Benjamin, he added, "tried to keep his acquaintances separate," notably the circles of his "German" as opposed to his Jewish interlocutors. One of Benjamin's secret sharers, of whom Scholem only became gradually aware as a potential mimetic rival during this early period of their friendship, was the (non-Jewish) poet, Fritz Heinle, with whom Benjamin had been very close during the pre-war years while active in Gustav Wyneken's youth movement. On August 8, 1914, the nineteen-year-old Heinle and his companion Rika Seligson asphyxiated themselves by turning on the kitchen gas in the meeting room of the Free Student Society of Berlin, of which Benjamin was a leading figure – a self-sacrificial protest against the juvenile enthusiasm that had greeted Germany's recent entry into the war.

Receiving Heinle's announcement of his planned suicide by telegram the following morning, Benjamin went into shock: this carefully premeditated act, committed by two of his closest friends, was – as he saw it – clearly an admonition addressed to him in person. He immediately severed all official contact with the youth movement and withdrew from any immediate political engagement with current events, preferring instead to view the war from the purely "metaphysical" or "theological" plane of absolute grief. Over the next six years, quitting Berlin for Munich and then taking up exile in Switzerland, Benjamin would secretly give himself up to the work of mourning Heinle in a series of seventy-three sonnets – rediscovered by Giorgio Agamben in 1981 and recently translated into English by Carl Skoggard. A dense amalgam of German baroque verse and the poetry of Hölderlin, Platen, George, and Rilke, Benjamin's hermetic *Sonnets* elevate Heinle into an angelic (and rather Christological) herald of the Night that had befallen the world in the wake of his luminous disappearance. Always unnamed, though addressed in the familiar Du (or Thou) form, Heinle figures as an absent presence, a *deus absconditus* ever to be mourned and resurrected and buried again in the Mallarméan tomb of verse – not unlike Stefan George's mystical adolescent muse, "Maximin." Scholem's diaries of this same period, composed while he was engaged in the translation of ancient Hebrew lamentations – though still unaware of his alter ego's secret sonnets – provide uncanny insights into Benjamin's elegiac brooding over his lost object: "The expression of lament is metaphysically conditioned by the elimination of an object's identity. All lamentation grieves that it loses its object, which thereby surrenders its metaphysical consistency and thus becomes expressionless. It is precisely the *countenance* of this process [i.e. the process of becoming faceless] that makes up the expression of lament. Screaming operates in similar ways… In a word, lamentation [elsewhere, he substitutes the word "translation"] is language at the point of disappearance."

Scholem first became fully cognizant of Benjamin's occult channeling of the dead Heinle upon receiving a copy of his 1917 essay on Dostoevsky's *The Idiot* (in which Prince Myshkin was described as "completely unapproachable, his life radiating an order whose center is precisely his own solitude, ripe to the point of disappearance"). Scholem's diary entry of November 15, 1917, written while he was studying at the University of Jena, registers his excited response: "Walter Benjamin's critique of *The Idiot* is shattering. What is the reason for this? Because lurking in the background is the figure of his dead friend. Benjamin has profoundly rediscovered in *The Idiot* the physiognomy of the youth movement's failure… Walter seems to have had the Teaching [*die Lehre*] transmitted to him from a teacher, namely, from his dead friend. He saw in him the essence of youth. He also saw how youth dies. It is unimaginable, monumental, how Walter Benjamin has survived the death of his friend. I'm breathless that he was able to give up his own youth (and this is the first miracle) and yet continue living with the *idea* of youth." Scholem shot off an impassioned letter to Benjamin with his reactions to the essay. Benjamin answered Scholem's missive with uncharacteristic frankness and warmth: his friend had seized, as no other could have, the "revelation" that lay hidden in his piece on *The Idiot*, given that its esoteric message was especially "addressed" to his privileged interpretation. Scholem called Benjamin's letter the "most perfect" he had ever received. He had at last been invited into the arcanum.

A month earlier, passing in review the previous two years of his life, Scholem had similarly written of his master in his diary: "Only as I had nearly found my way did the greatest experience in my life occur: I came into contact with a man of absolute and magnificent greatness. He exercised the deepest influence on my life – and not just through his Teaching but his essential being and the reverence I continue to feel for him till this very day. This man was not a Zionist, and it may be that he only came to Judaism through me. But he was the miracle that occurs only once in a generation. In him spoke out the deepest, most absolute Judaism – all without his having the foggiest idea that this was what he was doing.... Since then I know the truth of youth. He has taught me that we must give up our youth..." The Benjamin whom Scholem here idealizes (and whom he elsewhere compares to an "angel") has clearly taken on the features of his "dead friend" Heinle as a Teacher engaged in translating *die Lehre* from beyond the tomb – *Lehre* here understood by

Scholem as an (unwitting) transmission of the Torah. Benjamin therefore begins to assume for him the mantle of a Jewish "prophet of God," mournfully aware that the "youth" (or originating experience) of Zion has been irredeemably lost, while nonetheless holding out the hope for its messianic rejuvenation in some future present tense. Meanwhile, in these dark times, Benjamin's saintly mode of existence (which Scholem compares to that of a Hölderlin or Lao Tzu) proved that its advent could only be prepared through an exemplary discipline of silence, exile, and cunning.

In early January 1917, Scholem had been officially expelled from his father's house for his rebelliously anti-German Zionist activities. His brother Werner (who would later die at Buchenwald) was currently sitting in prison after his arrest as a left-wing agitator. In March, Scholem was summoned by his draft board, who decided he was now fit for military service despite his past history of deferments. By June, he found himself in a German army unit (assigned, appropriately enough, to post office duties). Meanwhile, Benjamin was writing him (coded) letters from Switzerland, encouraging him to jump ship for once and for all. Traumatized by the anti-Semitic coarseness of barracks life, Scholem proceeded to feign (so he later claimed) insanity. After having being diagnosed by the army doctors as suffering from delusional "dementia praecox" – Gerhard in fact had experienced moments in his adolescent past when he truly believed himself to be the new Messiah – he was consigned to a military psychiatric ward for a period of observation. Upon his medical discharge, he registered at the University of Jena for the fall semester, ostensibly to study mathematics, but where instead, still suffering from manic-depressive mood swings, he plunged into the translation of Hebrew lamentations and dirges. In a December 1917 diary entry, he admitted: "The power of the Hebrew compels me to such a degree that I irresistibly experience Hebrew even in the German language. My total lack of the *German* spirit of language, which I experience only as a transplant, may rightly be used to question the legitimate validity of my translation. Still, for me this translation remains a great act. I have borne witness to my love and to my present stage in life."

Who or what was the love to which Scholem was bearing witness in his lamentations? The very language of Hebrew in all its abyssal, unbridgeable silence? His irredeemable mourning for the lost object of Zion, still waiting to be redeemed? Or his current, unreciprocated passion for Greta Brauer (the sister of one of his oldest friends from the Young Judah youth group), in whose "purity" and moral sublimity he saw the ethical projection of the "absolute Judaism" of his friend Walter Benjamin – that other "midpoint" of his life? The latter had married Dora Pollak (née Kellner) in April 1917: Scholem first got to know the couple the previous summer, when he was invited for a stay in Dora's father's Bavarian villa, playing the co-conspirator in their nascent semi-adulterous affair (Walter was still engaged to another woman and Dora was not yet officially divorced from her husband). Dora's father happened to be the literary executor of the Zionist publicist Theodor Herzl, the subject of one of Scholem's earliest poems, and Dora herself, a translator from the English and political radical, was an intellectual presence not to be ignored. In Dora and Walter, Gerhard imagined the perfect hierogamic Jewish couple. For his birthday in December, 1917, they sent him photographs of each other. Scholem set up the images as a shrine in his student quarters at Jena, worshipping the two as the medium of his "post-assimilationist" salvation. When their son Stefan was born the following April, Gerhard wrote in his diary: "In this union everything deep and beautiful is joined into a living miracle."

At this point, Scholem had finally managed to obtain the necessary medical certificates establishing his purported mental illness, as well as a passport for a clinic in Switzerland where his malady (à la Hans Castorp) might eventually be cured. He was received with open arms by Walter and Dora in early May 1918 and installed in a small attic room next to their residence in Muri. Upon his arrival, momentarily leaving his translations of Hebrew lamentations to the side, Scholem composed a flurry of poems – German poems, most of them sonnets – directly or indirectly addressed to Benjamin. The latter had recently given him two sections of his essay "The Metaphysics of Youth" to read – "The Diary" and "The Ball." As was his habit with Benjamin's other writings, Scholem immediately made handwritten copies of them and then proceeded to transform their prose into poetry – or rather, into midrashic verse commentaries based upon his scribal transcriptions of the Torah of the master. In his piece on "The Diary," Benjamin – an admirer of Rilke's *Notebooks of Malte Laurids Brigge* – had analyzed the discontinuous temporality of journal writing as essential to the autobiographical construction (and destruction) of the "I" of youth. Scholem's exegetical "Paraphrase, from the Prose of 'The Diary'" is ostensibly addressed to the Thou of a female 'Belovèd" (no doubt the much-mourned Greta). Behind this apostrophe, however, also lies the figure of Benjamin (and behind him, the specter of Heinle) who had so haunted Gerhard's own diaries over the past three years:

You live alone in the diary of my life
Leading an immortal existence page by page
In death you have been given to me by Time
Lest I lose myself in you to things too great.

The final tercet of the sonnet deftly rephrases the dialectical reversals of time and identity that Benjamin had located within the always fragmentary, always broken present tense of *Tagebuch* writing:

The future was. The past shall be
The present shall untwain us before God
In this estrangement we shall be free.

"Estrangement" – *Entfremdung* in Scholem's German – here echoes Benjamin's pervasive use of the word *Abstand* throughout his essay on "The Diary." Literally a "standing away" or "standing off" from something or somebody, *Abstand* shades into the more general meaning of distance (or reserve). Rodney Livingstone, in his English translation of Benjamin's essay, chooses to convey the word as "interval" – that gap, that fissure, that caesura, that moment of non-coincidence which Benjamin describes as the defining structural feature of the diary (and indeed, of messianic time).

Except that Gerhard was finding it increasingly difficult to inhabit this interval. Seen up close in Muri, Walter and Dora began to lose their cultic aura and stood revealed as mere flawed mortals. In a diary entry of early June he wrote: "My life converges on suicide. Never have I considered death – death by my own hand – with so such immediacy as in these four weeks.... And Walter and Dora, instead of helping me, only make it worse... they are literally driving me to the grave... There are moments.... in which I consider them to be perfectly ignoble, especially in their behavior and their daily lives." He discovered in them an "element of decadence," an "amorality" and a "nihilism," particularly when it came to cynically mooching off the fortunes of their parents and in indulging materialistic, bourgeois luxury. The de-idealizing process seemed complete: "In three months these two people have turned me into an old man, a 'man of experience' who has seen more than he desires to. Even their truths are only accidental. They tell too many fibs…out of aesthetic pleasure, out of egotism, out of the need for leisure. Only gradually am I realizing how deceitful their lives are – also in their relationship to me."

Although Walter and Dora managed to dissuade Gerhard from killing himself in the course of an emotional late night discussion, they continued to play games with him. Later in that month of June he received a rather mischievous letter from their new baby Stefan (in Dora's hand) informing him "I believe you really know very little about my Papa." Scholem, deeply wounded and outraged, wrote a sonnet in reply to Stefan (i.e. to Dora) which he never sent. By the end of month, however, he had again managed to establish an *Abstand*, a distance from Benjamin: "I think that only from afar can a person have an absolute relationship with him…With him I have to keep silent about almost everything that gives me fulfillment…" He concluded in a lengthy diary entry of June 25th: "Basically he's *entirely* invisible, though he has opened himself up to me more than to anyone else who knows him. When all is said and done, his entire life is nothing more than one massive apology for his dead friend. Everything he does is nothing more than methodically taking the dark central point created by their friendship and lifting it up into *absolute* clarity. Every word he says about this genius proves this and also reveals his final intention: to make an accounting of himself to someone who is dead. I don't believe that since the prophets there has ever lived a man who has brought such a massive responsibility to completion. All of this occurs in utter invisibility. Instead of communicating himself, Walter insists that everyone see him, even though he hides himself. His method is completely unique. I can't put it any way other than the method of Revelation...."

Six days later, Benjamin finally agreed, for the very first time, to read Scholem his secret sonnets to Heinle, in the process rendering himself even more radiantly (in)visible: "Walter said afterwards: that this work, which he has been laboring on for three years, was and remains the reason for his complete loneliness, also toward me. He said he can have a connection only with people with whom he can discuss this. I'm the first person to learn about it. The sonnets are Revelations." It was shortly after this epiphany that Scholem wrote his most perfect poem to date, simply entitled "W. B." – a sonnet which he ceremoniously presented to Benjamin on his twenty-sixth birthday on July 15, 1918 (together with a draft of his comic University of Muri verse). The poem is worth quoting in its entirety. The idiom is Hölderlin's, lensed through Scholem's Benjaminian readings of the sonnets of Rilke and George. The mode is that of high Revelation, in which disclosure and concealment coincide in true (Hebraic) awe and silence:

> Mournful one, near to me yet ever remote,
> Only your calling holds you close to life
> But you do not speak. And the world is built
> on your silence. Mourning is the eternal dawn

You greet. And that you have not yet died
is a miracle that lies beyond my reach.
You simply are. And from your deep quiet
arises the question that binds us, each to each.

You who stood by me during my difficult days
are far from me who took you as his estate.
I must carry what I feel within me in silence.
For what you are going through is so great
that any words I might find to cast it in
would prove impure. Speech is thus a sin.

Benjamin may have felt embarrassed by the naked adulation of this sonnet, for he responded to Herr Gerhard's birthday gift through the intermediary of the infant angel Stefan, translated by Dora's hand: "There is actually no point in thanking you for your magnificent poem, for it's too beautiful for that. But when I'm bigger I'll probably write one to express my appreciation." Scholem would later confess in his diary: "I have written a lot of nonsense [about my relationship to Benjamin] in these pages, none of which is basically true – because one can only be silent about it. The sonnet I wrote for his birthday is the only time I've ventured into language."

After the intense months of family drama spent together at Muri during the spring and early summer of 1918, the triangular relationship between Gerhard, Walter, and Dora gradually eroded into further misunderstandings, offset by moments of rediscovered intellectual and emotional closeness. By late 1919, at war's end, Scholem had returned to Munich to pursue his Judaic studies (and to marry Escha Burchardt, a fellow student) while the Benjamins eventually resettled in Berlin, their circle of acquaintances now including figures for whom Scholem had little sympathy (such the conservative Protestant theologian Florens Christian Rang). Their marriage, moreover, was on the rocks, as Dora secretly confided to Gerhard. In an erotic chiasmus straight out of Goethe's *Elective Affinities,* she had fallen in love with one of Benjamin's oldest and closest friends, the musician Ernst Schoen, while Walter had become enamored of Jula Cohn, whom he had known from the Youth Movement (and who happened to be the sister of another longstanding school friend). It was in this state of disarray, dreaming of a *vita nuova* with Jula, that Walter (according to Scholem's 1972 essay, "Walter Benjamin and his Angel") purchased Paul Klee's oil monoprint "Angelus Novus" while visiting Munich in the spring 1921. Unable to hang it in Berlin – he was moving between residences, his marriage now on hold – Benjamin lent it to the Scholems for safekeeping in their apartment, where it was duly visited by Dora and her new lover Ernst Schoen in June and, shortly thereafter, by Walter, who stopped by on his way to Heidelberg to pursue his new angel and muse, Jula Cohn.

It was there that Benjamin received Scholem's poem "Greetings from Angelus" – an offering to him on his twenty-ninth birthday. This dramatic monologue, which evokes the (temporary) residence of Klee's painting on the wall of the Scholems' living room in Munich, is uttered in the voice of the Angel, speaking at once to Gerhard, his momentary landlord, and to Walter, his rightful owner. As in much of Scholem's poetry, the precise object and subject of angelic address remains oblique. The Angelus's salutation begins with the painting's stated aversion to the viewer's gaze:

> I hang nobly on the wall
> and look no one in the eye
> I've been sent from heaven
> an angelman am I.
>
> Man is well within my realm
> I take little interest in his case
> I am protected by the Almighty
> and have no need of face.

This indifference to the human, this refusal of representation lies at the core of Scholem's mystical understanding of the divine. Klee's modernist angel, however, is less a full-fledged symbol anchored in myth than a floating signifier:

> My gaze is never vacant
> my eye pitchdark and full
> I know what I must announce
> and many other things as well.
>
> I am an unsymbolic thing
> I mean what I mean
> you turn the magic ring in vain
> there is no sense to me.

Upon receiving the poem, Benjamin – who, in a standing joke, increasingly referred to himself by the name of "Angelus" in his correspondence with Scholem during this period – simply thanked him with the enigmatic comment: "The disadvantage of angel-language is that, despite its extraordinary beauty, one cannot reply to it."

While in Heidelberg, Benjamin was offered the editorship of a literary magazine by Richard Weissbach, the future publisher of his Baudelaire translations. He immediately decided to call the journal *Angelus Novus*, for as he explained in the prospectus he drew up for the venture, he hoped the title would, like Klee's inscrutable herald, announce "the new spirit of the age" and contribute to "the fate of the German language" by featuring "annihilatory" literary and philosophical criticism as well as new practices of translation, conceived of as "the strict and irreplaceable school of language-in-the-making." To this end, he planned to include in its pages the poems of the deceased Heinle and those of his younger brother Wolf, Scholem's translations from the Hebrew of the stories of S. Y. Agnon, an essay by Rang, and "The Task of the Translator," the theoretical introduction to his forthcoming Baudelaire volume. In addition, Benjamin turned to Scholem to secure submissions from such prominent Jewish figures as Ernst Lewy and Erich Unger – the latter an exponent of the doctrines of the messianic magus (or *Zauberjude*) Oskar Goldberg. Among much bitterness and back-stabbing, all these initiatives came to naught and Scholem, now caught up in his studies of ancient Hebrew and the Kabbalah, gradually backed out of the magazine, feeling that it was ultimately too "German" in its literary orientation.

It was at this juncture that in the late fall of 1921, back in Berlin, Benjamin finally sent a mischievous verse reply to Scholem's birthday "Greetings from Angelus" – here translated into English, I believe, for the first time. Its comic couplets simultaneously allude to the Klee that still hung on Gerhard's living room wall in Munich and to their arguments about which literary and religious direction the magazine *Angelus Novus* should take:

This fellow Scholem sends the Angelus
Away from his rightful locus
This grudging Gerhard thinks it wrong
That he go where he should belong
His wife Escha at his behest
Pretends to know nothing of the mess
For there in her living quarters
He's nailed to the wall like a poster
The Angelus there names himself *Engel*
Swiftly flying from strife this painful
For he does not like lingering in rooms
Of crafty wizard Jews

Benjamin insists on the German word for angel (*Engel* – not Engels), while teasing Scholem about bringing in "abgefeimten Zauber-Juden" ("crafty wizard Jews") such as Oskar Goldberg et. co. into the orbit of the journal.

The poem concludes with an allusion to the infant angel Stefan back in Berlin and to the recently published *Star of Redemption* by Franz Rosenzweig ("rose- branch"), in whose Judaic doctrine, Benjamin suggests, the Angel would prefer not to be permanently bedded down, choosing instead (unlike Scholem's poster child) to "hover," free from any religious message:

To find a home in Stefan's domicile
He diverts his radiant eye
One beds him down on a branch of roses
Whereas to hover is what he instead proposes

Two weeks later, Benjamin thanked Scholem for having dispatched the Klee back to Berlin, where it had taken its place above the sofa –

"although so far he has refused to provide us with any oracle-like whisperings in our ear." As for the journal *Angelus Novus*, Benjamin still held out hope for its publication, if only in ephemeral form. As he had observed in its prospectus: "After all, according to a legend in the Talmud, the angels – who are born anew every instant in countless numbers – are created in order to perish and to vanish into the void, once they have sung their hymn in the presence of God." As it turned out, *Angelus Novus* never even lived to see the light of print – a crushing disappointment.

Benjamin was committed to a cosmopolitan (and increasingly French) extension of German thought and letters, while Scholem was more and more inhabiting his own private Zion – to which he emigrated in 1923. From his new exilic home in Palestine, he again reached out to Benjamin in verse four years later, sending him a private printing of the Muri "Abecedarium" he had first presented to him on his birthday nearly a decade earlier; Benjamin jokingly thanked him for this homage to the "guardian angel" of their imaginary university. This was followed in 1933 by another one of Scholem's midrashic verse commentaries on his friend's writings – this time his autobiographical *One-Way Street*. Addressed to Kitty Marx (a close common friend), the poem evokes the shock-experiences encountered by the modern Berlin flâneur, and concludes by ventriloquizing Benjamin's post-Baudelairean voice (which I have rendered in alexandrines):

> We are not devout. Our domain is the profane,
> and where "God" once stood, Melancholy takes his place.

The "theological aspect of the world in which God does not appear" provided the bleak landscape in which Kafka's world was set – the subject of a lengthy Jerusalem-Paris exchange of letters between Scholem and Benjamin over the course of 1934, artfully analyzed by Robert Alter in his *Necessary Angel* of 1991. Scholem's most striking contribution to their argument was his "theological-didactic" poem, "With a Copy of Kafka's *Trial*," which he enclosed in a birthday letter to Benjamin of that year. Scholem counters Benjamin's absolutely nihilistic (and comic) readings of Kafka with a guarded (and rather solemn) messianic optimism:

> Are we utterly estranged from you?
> Lord, is no breath of your peace
> or hint of your promised light
> meant for us in this dark night?
>
> Can your word have become so faint
> among Zion's empty wastes –
> or has it yet to permeate
> the spellbound realm of semblance?
>
> The sheer illusion of the world
> is now consummated to the full.
> Lord, grant that he now may awake
> whom your absence has erased.
>
> This is the sole ray of revelation
> in an age that disavowed you,
> entitled only to experience you
> in the shape of your negation.

The quatrains echo those of the "Greetings from Angelus" that Scholem had sent Benjamin twelve years earlier – and to which he had never received an adequate reply. Receiving a fresh copy of the poem from Scholem in a 1933 letter, Benjamin was finally forced to admit: "I read your poem on the Angelus Novus again with undiminished admiration. I would place it among the best I know." In recognition of its melancholy power, he would later quote one of its quatrains as an epigraph to the ninth fragment of his late "Theses on the Philosophy of History," composed in 1940 while he was trapped in Paris, like Baudelaire's exiled swan:

> My wing is poised to beat
> I would gladly turn home
> were I to stay to the end of days
> I would still be this forlorn.

The ekphrastic prose poem that follows may be read as Benjamin's final message to Scholem—to whom he had already bequeathed his precious Klee in a suicide note of July, 1932. The damaged angel of this Ninth Thesis knows no redemption, no repair of broken vessels, no *tikkun*:

> There's a painting by Klee called "Angelus Novus." It depicts an angel who looks as if he were about to recoil from the object of his petrified gaze. His eyes are wide, his mouth agape, and his wings are spread. This is what the angel of history must look like. He has his face turned to the past. What we perceive as a chain of events, he sees as a single catastrophe, endlessly heaping ruin upon ruin and hurling the debris at his feet. He would gladly linger on – to wake the dead, to piece back together what has been shattered. But a storm is blowing from Paradise, so mighty that it has gotten caught in his wings and made it impossible for the angel to close them. The storm relentlessly buffets him into the future to which his back is turned, while the pile of debris before him mounts skyward. This storm is what we call progress.

After Benjamin took his own life at Port-Bou while unsuccessfully trying to cross the border into Spain in late 1940, Scholem seemed to lose confidence in his poetic voice, now bereft of its necessary angel. But

in a poem that he wrote about the curfew alarms in war-torn Jerusalem
of 1947, the angel briefly returned — now a member of that host of sirens
whose silence Kafka had been the first to hear:

> There are days when seeing your life
> resume its normal placid course,
> you hear their unexpected cry
> arise in lamentation, deep and hoarse,
>
> which, before reaching its highest pitch,
> gusts forth like a wild spring wind;
> and suddenly all the streets are thick
> with the interminable sound of groans
>
> whose unrelenting ups and downs
> heave you high onto steep waves
> of terror, then plunge you to the ground
> until your soul, torn apart, caves
>
> in. But then all the silence
> within the echo of these shrieks
> erupts, and your will goes weak,
> stunned by the horror of such stillness.
>
> Falling mute, they reduce you to a cower,
> as if covering you with blows,
> until one final monotonous moan
> at least releases you from their power.

Richard Sieburth
September 11, 2017

WORKS CONSULTED:

Robert Alter, *Necessary Angels: Tradition and Modernity in Kafka, Benjamin and Scholem* (Cambridge: Harvard University Press, 1991)

Walter Benjamin, *Early Writings 1910-1917*, translated by Howard Eiland et. al. (Cambridge: Harvard University Press, 2011)

Walter Benjamin, *Gesammelte Schriften, Briefe*, Band 1-2 (Frankfurt: Surhkamp, 1978)

Walter Benjamin, *Selected Writings 1913-1926*, edited by Marcus Bullock and Michael W. Jennings (Cambridge: Harvard University Press, 1996)

Walter Benjamin, *Sonnets*, translated and with commentary by Carl Skoggard (Quebec: Pilot Editions, 2014)

Howard Eiland and Michael W. Jennings, *Walter Benjamin: A Critical Life* (Cambridge: Harvard University Press, 2014)

George Prochnik, *Stranger in a Strange Land: Searching for Gershom Scholem and Jerusalem* (New York: Other Press, 2016)

Gershom Scholem, *A Life in Letters 1914-1982*, edited and translated by Anthony David Skinner (Cambridge: Harvard Univeristy Press, 2002)

Gershom Scholem ed., *The Correspondence of Walter Benjamin and Gershom Sholem 1932-1940*, translated by Gary Smith and André Lefevere (New York: Schocken Books (1989)

Gershom Scholem, *Lamentations of Youth: The Diaries of Gershom Scholem 1913-1919*, edited and translated by Anthony David Skinner (Cambridge: Harvard University Press, 2007)

Gershom Scholem, "Walter Benjamin and his Angel," in Gary Smith editor, *On Walter Benjamin: Critical Essays and Recollections* (Cambridge: MIT Press, 1988)

Gershom Scholem, *Walter Benjamin: The Story of a Friendship*, translated by Harry Zohn (New York: Schocken Books, 1981)

is a not-for-profit literary press devoted to
promoting cross-cultural exchange through innovative
classic and contemporary international literature
www.archipelagobooks.org